Bill Dance on

LARGEMOUTH BASS

By Bill Dance

with

Tim Tucker

 A TIM TUCKER OUTDOOR PRODUCTION

BOOKS BY BILL DANCE

Bill Dance on Crappie
Bass'N Tips
Bass'N Objects
Practical Black Bass Fishing
There He Is
Bass Fishing Techniques

BOOKS BY TIM TUCKER

Diary of a Bass Pro
Secrets of America's Best Bass Pros
More! Secrets of America's Best Bass Pros
Doug Hannon's Fisherman's Logbook
Roland Martin's 101 Bass-Catching Secrets
Advanced Shiner Fishing Techniques
Bill Dance on Crappie

To Bryan Kerchal, who left us too soon.

Printed in the United States of America by
Atlantic Printing
P.O. Box 67
Tabor City, NC 28463

ISBN Number 0-937866-53-9
Library of Congress Card No. 95-090837

Cover design by Tom Scott Designs, Suite B-1506 McCallie Ave.,
Chattanooga, TN 37404 (615-622-1875).

Cover photo by Scott Liles. Inside photos by Scott Liles, Gerald
Crawford, Bill Dance and Tim Tucker

About the Authors

Bill Dance is one of America's best-loved fishermen and an icon of the television fishing scene. After a highly successful  tournament career that included eight Bass Anglers Sportsman Society tournament victories and two Angler of the Year awards, he retired in 1980 to pursue a career in television. His highly popular Bill Dance Outdoors is one of the most successful and longest-running fishing shows of all time. It is seen weekends on The Nashville Network. In addition to being a columnist for North American Fisherman and Bassin' magazines, Dance is a popular seminar speaker, educator, book author, columnist for several newspapers and host of a 60-market daily radio show sponsored by Bryan Meats. He is a member of the International Fishing Hall of Fame.

Bill and wife Dianne live in Eads, Tenn.

Tim Tucker is one of the country's most published outdoor writers and winner of more than 100 awards for his  writing and photography. In addition to being a senior writer for BASSMASTER Magazine, B.A.S.S. Times and Southern Outdoors, his work has appeared in Field & Stream, Fishing Tackle Retailer, Southern Saltwater, Crappie, Florida Sportsman, Bass Fishing, Florida Wildlife, Bassin', North American Fisherman, Advanced Bass Strategies, Bass Pro Shops Outdoor World, Fishing Facts and numerous other publications. The outdoors writer for the Gainesville Sun newspaper, the veteran angler/writer has authored eight books on fishing, including the popular Secrets of America's Best Bass Pros and More! Secrets of America's Best Bass Pros. He owns and operates a book publishing, audio production and merchandise catalog company.

Tim and wife Darlene live in Micanopy, Fla.

Acknowledgements

The authors would like to thank Dianne Dance, Scott Liles, Darlene Tucker, Bruce Benedict, Tom Scott, Gary Giudice, Gary Walker, Patti Taylor, Tony Mack, Al Linder (of In-Fisherman fame), Mark Sosin, Julie Bailey, Steve Persinger and John Pepper for helping make this book a reality.

Special thanks to Bernie Schultz and Jim Farrior, a pair of talented illustrators and anglers whose work helped bring this book to life.

And, finally, there is the largemouth itself — the largest member of the sunfish family, the fish known scientifically as Micropterus salmoides and less formally as the black bass.

The inherent genetic qualities of this species deserves the most credit of all. Over the years, this fish has displayed an amazing ability to adapt to all sorts of water conditions — even the once-polluted waters of the historic Potomac River.

That has enabled the species to flourish in every state of the union, except for Alaska and certain areas of the Rocky Mountain and Great Plains states (it is even thriving in sugarcane plantation lakes in Hawaii). The largemouth has adapted to every type of water including rivers, natural lakes, man-made reservoirs, stripped-down phosphate pits, tidal waters, small farm ponds, enormous bodies of water like Florida's Lake Okeechobee, roadside ditches, brackish coastal tributaries where fresh and saltwater mix, tropical swamps and iced-over northern lakes.

No lake, it seems, can be too artificial for the largemouth bass. Lake Castaic, that California big-bass haven mentioned earlier, is a prime example. To create Castaic, the water lords simply picked out a canyon arm in the desert, built a dam and piped in water from the Sacramento River (a whopping 300 miles away) via aqueduct. Add bass (which are not native to California) and you have the beginnings of a great fishery.

But you wouldn't know it to look at this lake located in the shadow of Los Angeles. Let your mind drift and you could easily picture yourself fishing on the moon as you are surrounded by the stark, hilly shoreline with absolutely no trees or brush. Believe it or not, there are even four floating portable toilets anchored around this fake lake. Talk about a foreign land...

The successful creation of lakes like Castaic illustrates what an adaptable creature we have in the largemouth bass.

Further evidence can be seen in the wide variety of foreign countries where largemouths have been transplanted. The list includes Canada (home to some excellent fishing in its natural lakes), Mexico (we all know about these exotic lakes where trophy bass are plentiful), Africa (especially in Zimbabwe), South and Central America and Asian countries like the Philippines and Japan. Japanese anglers have a voracious appetite for anything that has to do with bass fishing, which just might be the country's most popular sport. The Japanese are avid tackle buyers who are crazy about tournament fishing and the stars of the B.A.S.S. Tournament Trail.

Some of the species' best qualities that I mentioned earlier in this chapter combine to make largemouth the fish that more fishermen target than any other in the United States. Those qualities are

Recycling efforts like Florida guide Dan Thurmond's tag-and-release practice is a big reason why our fishing is universally good these days.

the reason why the participation is so huge nationwide and an organization like B.A.S.S. has grown to more than 650,000 members in 50 states (including bass-starved Alaska) and 50 countries.

That popularity extends into every region of the country. Fishing for largemouth bass has long been practically a cradle-to-grave ritual in the South. Today, that same fever is growing rapidly in the Northeast, Southwest and Midwest.

Of course, what's not to like about a fish that can be caught by old folks and young kids alike on anything from cane poles to down-riggers?

I think the main reason why the largemouth is such a popular quarry (in addition to the qualities previously mentioned) is that this sporty species is most often found in shallow water. These fish spend most of their lives relating to visible targets in shallow water and are opportunistic hunters who are just as likely to annihilate a topwater plug as they are to pick up a bottom-hugging jig on any given day.

Casting to shallow, obvious targets is the way most of America likes to fish. And the largemouth is the marauding creature they would most like to catch.

And there is one final aspect of bass and bass fishing that is dear to the hearts of largemouth anglers everywhere. Tournament fishermen have taught us that regardless of the conditions, season or location, there is always a way that a bass can be caught.

Take heart in that the next time you venture out in search of America's favorite gamefish.

CHAPTER 2

THE BASICS OF BASS BEHAVIOR

Any bass enthusiast knows that the key to locating and catching bass begins with understanding the basic behavioral instincts and patterns of the largemouth itself.

There is no doubt about it, bass behavior is always changing, and that is due to the weather, water, and food conditions that are constantly changing. These changes significantly affect the fish's mood and activity level.

This is why it's so important for an angler to be as versatile as possible. He must analyze the conditions and make a decision about where the fish are and what they will hit best.

I know this is why good fishermen are more successful — because they have gained a tremendous amount of experience, which greatly helps in making good decisions. But like I've said many, many times, the more you go, the more you will learn and, in time, you will add to your knowledge and learn to make the correct moves faster.

Every time you go, one thing that affects your fishing is the weather. Many times it will help you and other times it will hurt you. Experienced fishermen recognize this and take advantage of good conditions — and work around unfavorable ones. It is a well-known fact that bass are very sensitive to changes in weather, such as a cold front, wind shifting direction and rising or falling barometric pressure, to mention a few. But these are some of the things you will gradually notice and figure out the more you try.

Bass fishing is such a challenging sport. There are always factors that are going to affect fish behavior. The fish's world is constantly changing. There is always something going on down there. But experience and time will help you more than you will ever believe.

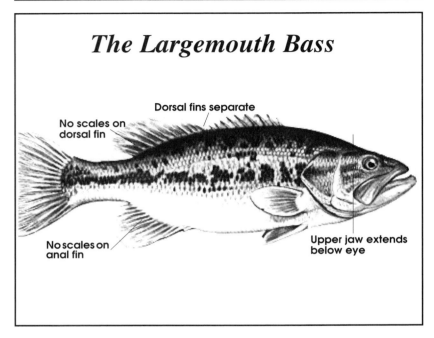

The Largemouth Bass

Dorsal fins separate

No scales on dorsal fin

No scales on anal fin

Upper jaw extends below eye

THE BASS' HOME RANGE

Let me tell you something you might find interesting. Anglers have disagreed for years on whether or not largemouth bass exhibit a home-range tendency. That is, when the bass move into the shoreline, do they continue to occupy the same relative place repeatedly? Or do they pick new sections of shoreline at random, based on where they happen to be at the moment? Studies by biologists have shown that bass do have a home range. Two scientists studied the bass population in a lake in Illinois and came to the same conclusion. The technique they employed was to cover the shoreline in a boat and (using electrical shocking equipment) capture the bass using shoreline cover. The fish were then marked for identification and returned to the water unharmed. Over the course of several months, the procedure was repeated a number of times and records were kept of where each tagged bass was found.

One of the more interesting facts to come from this study was that only 1.2 percent of the bass were on the shoreline at any one time on the average. That meant that most of the bass population — over 98 percent — was out from the shoreline or in deeper water the majority of the time. Recaptures indicated that 96 percent of the bass that did invade the shallows or shoreline were again found within 300 feet of the spot where they were first captured and marked for identification. With some bass, recapture took place three or four times. Yet they were always within the same area. After wintering in deep water, the same bass returned to the same segment of shoreline.

So the next time you locate a productive area, make a mental note of it. If the conditions are about the same the next time you are in the area, fish that spot again (even if it is a week, a month, or even a year later). You really might be surprised at what you find.

THE 'FINS' GAME

Millions of bass and bass fishermen have come into contact with each other over the years. But I'm willing to bet that few anglers have given much thought to the various fins on a largemouth and what purpose they serve.

Do you know the names of the fins on a bass and exactly how they are used? Well, I'll try to explain their function.

The bass uses his fins primarily for stability, maneuvering and various other special tasks. In fact, a bass usually retracts its fins when it wants to speed up — dropping them back against its body so that they virtually disappear.

The pectoral fins are used as planners when extended, enabling the bass to dive (if the fins are tipped down). If they are tipped up, that allows the bass to climb. They can also be extended one at a time to help the fish turn right or left, as well as back up.

The pelvic fins play a similar, but less important role.

The dorsal, the soft ray dorsal and anal fins are used mainly as keels to eliminate rocking motion, as well as keeping the fish straight up while swimming (particularly at slow speeds). At fast speeds, a bass is able to maintain a balanced course without much help from these fins.

The tail fin allows for forward movement, maneuverability and speed.

The fins not only promote fast starts and rapid turns, but also permit quick stops when both the pectorals and pelvic fins are thrust out suddenly. One final thing you might like to know, is that a bass has bursts of speed of 12 miles per hour and can swim approximately 7 miles per hour for each foot of its length. That is impressive.

BASS VISION

Ichthyologists and biologists both have found through years of research that a bass' eye receives five times more light than a human eye. Their eyes gather more light and, in effect, amplify it — allowing them to see at much lower light levels than we can (as well as at much greater distances).

Scientists say that fish can see over 40 feet in relatively clear water. In scuba gear, we can see approximately 10 to 12 feet. In stained water where we can see 2 to 4 feet, tests show that large-mouths can see up to 14 to 16 feet. And in a muddy environment where we can see only 6 inches or so, bass can somehow still see 3 to 5 feet.

It is a well-known fact that water absorbs some light rays faster than others — therefore changing the appearance of colors as man or a camera sees them. But remember that a bass' eyes are different than ours. Although researchers don't really know how fish perceive color, they do know which colors are most effective for catching fish in different light levels and water clarity. The way they know this is by using a device that took over nine years to complete. The device is a Color-C-Lector and was invented by a close friend of mine, Dr. Loren Hill, chairman of the Zoology Department at the University of Oklahoma. This unit definitely takes the guesswork out of what color is most visible to the fish at different times of the day, depth and water clarity. This unit also will give you the temperature and pH of the water from the surface down to 50 feet. It is a valuable piece of equipment to have.

Since a bass' eyes are on the sides of its head, it has a wide range of sight. However, the right and left eyes each see a separate half of the field, so they suffer a little from split vision. Nevertheless, it is an advantage to have each eye able to scan an arc of 180 degrees or more on each side of the body.

To the fish's rear, there is a definite blind spot where neither eye can see. This is why, you will always catch more fish by bring-

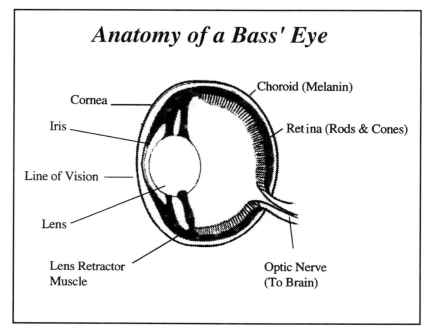

Anatomy of a Bass' Eye

Cornea

Iris

Line of Vision

Lens

Lens Retractor
Muscle

Choroid (Melanin)

Retina (Rods & Cones)

Optic Nerve
(To Brain)

ing your lure to the fish rather than bringing it up behind it. This will startle bass and spook them away. From dead ahead, a fish can see your bait at a distance and react to it quicker. Also, from straight ahead, the arcs of the two eyes overlap to provide a narrow band, perhaps 45 degrees, where the fish has binocular vision.

It is in this band of binocular vision that a fish can be expected to have accurate depth perception. In chasing down an artificial lure or living prey where depth perception is important, bass will attack straight ahead, because this straight-on positioning gives a fish the maximum ability to estimate target distance. Without depth perception, a bass has a tough time estimating the range of its target and hitting the mark. And if the lure or prey is not too visible, the fish's chances of getting it are virtually nil — regardless of what direction it is moving.

When fishing moving water, most fishermen know that it is always best to cast upstream. Bass are always facing upstream in a current to meet oncoming food. Fishing this way allows you to work the lure much more effectively and in more of a natural way. When you cast, try for a head-on shot at the bass, as opposed to bringing your lure at them from the sides.

To more clearly understand how largemouth bass see, picture this: there is a wedge in front of the bass where the visual fields of both eyes overlap. Binocular vision lets them zero in on their prey so they can strike accurately. When something goes across their field of vision, it is visible to them for a much shorter time than if it is either going away or coming straight for them.

As a result, it is always best to cast your lure so that it comes straight toward the anticipated position of the bass.

Sound or smell might lead the fish to your bait, but the final attack is dictated by sight in almost every instance. Therefore, if you can get a lure in front of the bass in a natural manner — and it is approximately the correct shape, size and color — you will have increased your odds for success tremendously.

FEEDING AND FOOD PREFERENCES

In order to survive, a largemouth soon learns to measure the amount of energy it expends in relation to the rewards received. If a bass must expend more energy to catch its prey than the nourishment value provided by the forage species, it just isn't worth the effort.

When you cast around an object like a stump, for instance, you should realize that the bass will usually strike the lure when it comes close to it — rather than chase the bait right up to the bank or back to the boat. There are exceptions of course, but you can waste a lot of fishing for the exception. A better approach is to fish the object carefully, slowly, and then retrieve rapidly for the next cast.

All predators exhibit a number of general tendencies. Two of the most important involve feeding in a school of baitfish. Contrary to the belief of some fishermen, a bass does not merely open its mouth and crash through a school of baitfish in a random manner. In order to strike and feed effectively, a largemouth must isolate a specific victim and then pursue it for the best results. At the same time, a fish is more prone to select a prey that appears disabled or looks different from the others.

These principles are particularly significant when bass are feeding on a school of baitfish. And they help to explain why bass will strike a lure that lands amid the baitfish and then is retrieved out of the school. The instant the lure clears the school, it is easy for a bass to isolate it and attack. It looks somewhat different from the other fish in the school and, by adding erratic or crippled action to your lure, it will really stand out from the crowd.

Bass are general predators who prefer live or artificial food that looks and acts alive. Their diet varies, but they will often become very selective and will specialize for feeding efficiency. For example, if a lake is loaded with 2- to 3-inch threadfin shad, the bass may prefer to feed on these — ignoring other foods in the process — except for one particular creature.

Research has shown that mature bass display a decided preference for the most prevalent forage found in our lakes, ponds, sloughs, creeks and rivers — the crawfish. And for good reason. Bass feeding on crawfish grow much faster than those that don't live where crawfish are abundant. Another reason is that crawfish are much easier to catch, therefore the bass expend less energy and gain the high protein that this forage provides. If you are looking for bass and find crawfish in the area, the chances are good that the fish will be close by.

Have you ever wondered why baitfish bunch up so tightly? It is simply for survival, a defensive mechanism. By gathering closely together, they create a large image that looks like a big fish. Even the movement of a school creates the impulse sounds of a large fish. But perhaps their defensive scheme is most often spoiled by the odor that all baitfish emit into the water that is detected by the keen sense of smell that bass possess. Many times, you will be able to spot submerged schools of baitfish by the oil slick that appears on the surface from the natural discharge of the forage. It is very important to be observant. If the school of baitfish are moving quickly downwind, the oil slick would appear upwind. Naturally, if the concentration is milling in one area, the wind current would drift the slick below them. Often, you will be able to detect the location of the baitfish with polarized glasses. Sometimes they will appear as dark areas below the surface; other times you will be able to spot the actual school by the surface movement created by a single baitfish. And when they are deeper, your depthfinder will tell you the location, depth and direction that the forage is moving.

BAROMETRIC PRESSURE AND BASS

I honestly believe that the main reason largemouth bass are such a challenging gamefish is because they seem to be more influenced by environmental changes than other species.

Nearly everything that happens in the air and in the water has an effect on most freshwater gamefish, especially largemouth bass. Normally two or more fluctuating conditions are in effect at the same time — simply because they are all related — and everything that happens in the atmosphere eventually affects the watery world of fish.

Barometric pressure has a dramatic influence on bass and other fish.

In all of my years of fishing, one of the key things I've noticed (particularly about shallow water fishing) is the dramatic influence that barometric pressure has on fish. Ironically, this is the one influence that biologists, ichthyologists and serious fishermen have studied least. This could be because the required equipment is so delicate that it is difficult to take to the lake. And the whole pressure equation really gets complicated when you try to measure it against water pressure, which also changes as fish change depth.

It is a well-known fact that even minor barometric pressure changes affect a bass' swim bladder. This air-filled sac is to a fish what the inner ear is to humans. When the barometric pressure rises quickly, it exerts pressure upon the bladder, thus affecting the fish's equilibrium — making it hard for the bass to maintain perfect balance. Naturally, this affects their behavior and appetite.

I'm sure you've heard the term "barometric pressure" many times, but do you know what it actually means? Simply stated, it is the pressure of the atmosphere at a given point and time. And it's measured by a barometer, which is an instrument for determining the pressure of the atmosphere and predicting probable weather changes.

About 10 years ago, I started watching the barometer very closely. I had a cheap version that worked fairly well, but just to be sure I would also check with the local weather service before and after every trip. This improved my understanding of how pressure fluctuations affect bass behavior.

All serious bass fishermen know that the barometric pressure has a dramatic and immediate effect on a fish's personality and mood. Without question, it is an important element that influences fish behavior, especially shallow-water bass. Deep-water fish are not affected as much by major pressure changes and this is why they are more dependable on those days.

Something to keep in mind is that barometric pressure doesn't change dramatically during a period of just a few hours, unless a major storm is moving your way.

Like fish, other wildlife can predict the weather better than The Weather Channel or the National Weather Service. Mother Nature has given her creatures the uncanny ability to accurately anticipate an approaching weather system, as well as knowing how long it will last.

As a general rule, I concentrate my efforts in shallower water during falling pressure and in deeper water when it rises. Normally, barometric fluctuations are most important during late-fall, winter, and early to mid-spring (because that is when fronts that frequently move from both the northwest and due north are the strongest). Fronts that occur during the summer and early fall seem to move more from the southwest or west, and have less effect. Plus, the recovery time is much quicker during these warmer periods of the year.

A lot of folks think that the perfect day to be fishing is a beautiful day when the sun is out, the sky is blue, and there's not a cloud to spoil the view. But let me tell you, most of the time these are the worst conditions for catching fish, because these conditions normally prevail just after a front has passed through. This is the type day when the pressure goes up and up — and the bass either go down or move into thick cover and seem to get lockjaw. When these conditions occur, you have to really slow down and use lures that you can work extremely slow (those that appear less likely to escape). Worms, grubs, or jig-and-pork combinations are good choices.

How many times have you heard fishermen say "Wind out of the east, fish bite the least. Wind out of the west, fish bite the best." Or " Wind out of the north, don't venture forth." And "Winds out of the south, blows the bait in the fish's mouth." Well, first of all, the direction of the wind doesn't directly affect fishing. I've caught fish in wind of all directions, except when it was blowing so hard I couldn't get out, or perhaps when it was too strong to fish a particular area. However, there is some truth about the effects of wind direction which actually has its roots in the barometric pressure. That's right, it deals with fronts. A strong brisk north or east wind will generally indicate a fast weather change and, therefore, a drastic change in barometric pressure. Gusty south or west winds usually indicate a slowly changing weather condition and thus minor changes in the pressure. So it's not really that the wind affects fish behavior. Instead, it's the barometric pressure that affects the wind and, therefore, fish behavior.

I think it would be safe to say that most fishermen can remember times when they were really whacking the fish and, all of a sudden, the wind changed direction and the fish stopped biting. This happens often, but, again, it's not actually the wind that makes the difference. A dramatic shift in wind direction is the result of a frontal passage or change in barometric pressure.

If I've said this once, I've said it a thousand times: the best time to go fishing is any time you can go. But if you can schedule your trips to coincide with the best weather forecast for current conditions, it will certainly pay you to do so because this is when the fish will be the most active.

Let me take a minute to explain what my experience has been with different ranges of pressure — both the good and the bad. Where I live in west Tennessee, our normal pressure is 30 inches of mercury. So naturally, any reading below 30 is low and any above 30 is high. An optimum range would be 29.98 to 30.02. Without question, some of my best catches and biggest fish have come from mid-spring to early fall after several days of normal pressure were interrupted by an approaching front that caused the pressure to fall extremely fast (more than 10 to 15 points) in a few hours time. Normally during such a period, you will see bad weather moving your way, and the bass will go on a feeding frenzy. Generally, these feeding sprees are short lived and to take maximum advantage of them, you have to take the unsafe risk of possible high winds and lightning.

I would say that the next best time for me would be a couple of days after the front has passed (especially in the winter). The wind shifts back to the south or west and the pressure slowly begins to settle back to normal. Another good period is when the pressure has been steady for several days.

Now, the worst pressure condition for me is when the barometer reading is below 29.90 or above 30.20. High pressure can have just as much effect on most shallow water gamefish as low pressure does. You might tend to think that the day after a front — a bright, sunny, bluebird day — would be a great day for fishing. On the contrary, it is the worst for me, especially during late-fall to early spring. During the colder water periods, recovery time can take as much as three to four days before the action begins to pick up again. Normally during the summer months, recovery time is considerably shorter.

There are many things that affect fish behavior — water quality, water temperature, water pH, water clarity, water fluctuation, just to mention a few. But of all these, barometric pressure rates right up at the top as far as I'm concerned.

CHAPTER 3

TASTE AND SMELL

Have you ever wondered just how sensitive a bass' sense of smell is?

From what we are beginning to learn, it is much more sensitive than anglers realize. Scientific research shows that some fish can be drawn to a chemical source from several hundred yards away. In addition, studies indicate that fish can recognize aquatic plants and even other fish in their same school by their individual smell. It has also been documented that a bass' ability to smell is so incredible that it can smell a thousand times better than a dog. A dog's sense of smell is about a thousand times better than a human's.

This alone tells me just how important the sense of smell is in a fish's life.

Scientific studies on some species, including largemouth bass, have found that the olfactory area in which a fish smells doubles or triples in size as the fish grows old. This finding leaves researchers to speculate that older and larger bass have a better developed sense of smell.

Maybe this is one of the key reasons why big fish are harder to catch.

My good friend, professor Mike Howell, head of the Department of Biology at Samford University, states that the fish's astounding sense of sound and taste has been underestimated by almost all fishermen. We humans with our poorly developed senses of smell and taste find it really hard to identify adequately in human terms about the fantastic keen senses in fish. Realizing the importance of taste, I honestly feel smell is much more important.

Example: If a fish can taste from a distance, then what good is the sense of smell? Smell is more long range and detects a wider variety of substances. Bass typically use taste as a nearby or contact sense. They also use taste more selectively than smell. A bass may be drawn from several yards away by the smell of forage, but it will

Fishing partner Gary Dollahan of Zebco understands the positive impact of a fish attractant and balanced tackle.

not rely on taste until it mouths it. Naturally, if it doesn't taste good, more times than not the fish is going to reject it.

Different species of fish have different food preferences. What a largemouth might enjoy eating might cause a walleye to look for a bottle of Maalox. The closer the biological relationship between two species, the more common their food preference is. Still, what a sunfish enjoys might not be enjoyable to his big cousin, the bass. In many cases, taste and smell seem to be species-specific.

Have you ever wondered why some species of fish prefer certain foods? Why some are picky eaters, while others wolf down everything they can get their mouth on. Well, research has shown there are two parts to this answer — instinctive taste preference and conditioning.

Instinctive taste preferences is one part.

A crappie doesn't care much for crawfish. Sure, it might try a few if it was starving to death. But crappie have other preferences like small baitfish. Some species instinctively like and dislike certain flavors and odors. Ichthyologists don't understand why — that's just how they are. It's kind of like people who wdon't like certain foods.

The other part of that answer is conditioning.

A bass, however, loves crawfish, which have their own distinctive odor and taste. Over time, bass have learned that these little creatures are good to eat. Could it be that it's the favorite food of a bass? Maybe yes, maybe no, but because of acceptable taste, availability, a positive feeding experience, the bass continues to devour them. People, animals, and fish tend to repeat things that turn out well.

Just as certain smells and flavors attract a positive response from the fish, certain odors repel fish, and are very distasteful to fish (such as insect repellent, human scent, tobacco products and sunscreens). Another interesting note: because of a fish's acute sense of smell and taste, many components on a fishing lure can be a repellent. Hooks, metals, plastic, wood and paint all give off odors that fish can smell. It is smart to mask all odors whenever possible.

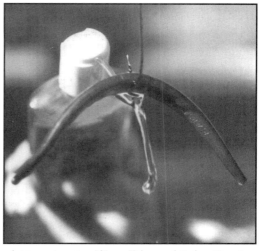

Attractants like Riverside's Real Baitfish can entice and encourage bass behavior.

A product like No-o-dor instantly removes all foreign taste and smell on lures. This product will oxidize the organic molecules that a fish detects before striking. After applying and removing all distasteful odors and smell, it is smart then to add an attractant, like Riverside's scents, especially on slow-moving baits like plastic lizards, grubs, worms and the jig-and-pork combination.

The more a bait looks, tastes and smells natural, the greater the catch rate. I'm sure you have seen a bass follow a lure and then turn away just when you thought it was gonna blast it. More times than not, the fish smelled or tasted something unusual. Many lures have an unnatural synthetic scent. They taste and smell like plastic, not a natural forage. By adding an attractant, the fish will be more enticed to strike and hold it in its mouth longer, allowing for more time to set the hook.

Many fishermen overlook the importance of taste and smell. The scientific evidence today strongly suggests that fish attractants can have a positive impact on your catch rate. If you use them properly, fish attractants can entice and encourage fish behavior in many species of gamefish.

I'll be the first to tell you, that such attractants are not a magic potion or cure-all. They cannot compensate for improper lure selection, presentations or produce fish where there are none. But they can and will improve your chances of success, in a mighty big way.

Like I said earlier, smell and taste are key senses, but smell in my opinion is more important. Why? Well as I stated a few minutes ago, smell is always associated with the fish's nostrils, and taste is normally associated with the taste buds around the mouth area.

The smell and taste nerves go to different parts of the bass' brain, which means that smell is a more long-range or distant sense, while taste is a contact sense. Example: a fish may be drawn from several yards away by a particular smell of a food item, however, it doesn't taste it until it is in its mouth and by then, it is normally too late.

Finally, let me say once more that there is proven evidence to show that the sense of smell is incredibly involved in a fish's life. And this is why you'll improve your catches, by adding a fish attractant to your lure — especially when fish are inactive. And when you really think about it, bass are largely inactive the majority of times that we fish.

CHAPTER 4

THE IMPORTANCE OF SOUND

Of all the sensory systems of a bass, hearing is perhaps the most versatile. Even when vision is obscured as the clarity of water changes, the days turn to darkness, or the clear body of water flows into mud, the hearing functions of bass adapt and remain extremely sharp. This system is so precise that it enables a bass to hear sounds we cannot hear. And most of these sounds trigger a reaction.

One type of sound will signal the approach of a baitfish. Another may arouse curiosity. Fear, brought about by other sounds, may send the bass to deeper water or the safety of the nearest cover. Because sounds do affect bass, that knowledge can be put to good use by fishermen.

Basically, sounds transmitted into the water can either repel or attract bass. The trick, of course, is to avoid driving them away with the wrong kind of sound and instead to arouse their curiosity or gain their attention with the right type of sound.

We know that sound travels five times faster in the water than it does in air. And we also are aware that bass are extremely sensitive to a wide range of frequencies. Interestingly enough, you will seldom see a bass make a mistake and charge toward an alarming sound. The fish immediately moves away from it. Yet, a lure with an attractive sound will sometimes make it charge forward without any hesitation (provided the correct presentation is made).

One mistake many beginning fishermen make is casting directly alongside or on top of cover where the bass is lying. Unfortunately, the angler seldom sees the results of his efforts. A better approach is to cast beyond your target if possible and then cover that area during the retrieve.

As stated earlier, it's important to remember that sound travels five times faster in water than it does in the air (at a rate of approximately one mile per second). Because water is an excellent

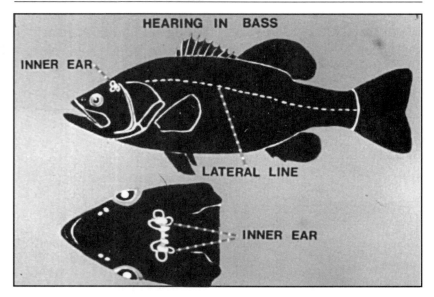

Unlike humans, bass do not have eardrums and their ears are not open to the water on the outside. Sounds are transmitted through the skin, flesh and bone of the bass' head to the ears.

conductor of sound waves, but a very poor transmitter of light waves, bass have been blessed with an exceptionally good sense of hearing.

Although bass don't have earflaps like we do, they do have ears and good ones. The hearing apparatus of a bass is a highly developed sense organ that is so sensitive that it can sense the noise of a crawfish moving about under a rock.

A bass' ears are buried on either side of its head, in roughly the same position in which our own inner ears are found, but much closer together. Unlike us, bass do not have eardrums and their ears are not open to the water on the outside. Sounds are transmitted directly from the water though the skin, flesh and bone of the bass' head to the ears.

Ichthyologists claim that one clue to extremely sensitive hearing in certain species like the bass, is an internal connection between the ear and the swim bladder. Because the swim bladder is a gas-filled chamber enclosed by an elastic membrane, it serves as an underwater microphone and amplifier all rolled into one. The bladder picks up vibrations from the water and transmits them directly to the ear.

There's no doubt about it, high sensitivity hearing is a valuable asset to the hunted as well as the hunter.

Knowing how sensitive hearing is to a bass, you might be wondering how important is sound that is carried in the air, like a normal conversation between fishermen. Well, this doesn't affect bass at all, simply because the water's surface reflects 99.9 percent of the sound energy in the air.

Something you might find interesting is that bass not only "hear" sounds, but they "feel" sounds. A bass hears high-frequency sound waves through the inner ear and feels low-frequency sound waves through its lateral line.

At approximately 40 feet, high-frequency sound waves from a lure reach the bass' inner ear. However, the bass may not be able to clearly distinguish or identify the sound of the lure at this distance, simply because of other underwater sounds traveling through the water. At a distance less than 20 feet, the bass relies on both the inner ear and heavily on the lateral line. Since the lateral line is directional, a bass can detect and sense the direction of a lure quite well.

Some scientists refer to the lateral line as the "sense of distance touch." It is almost as if a bass could reach out and feel.

Bass can locate sounds in a restricted range using the lateral line detector. At distances beyond 20 feet, they detect sounds with the inner ear, but cannot locate the source without swimming a search pattern or until the sounds come closer. Once the sound is

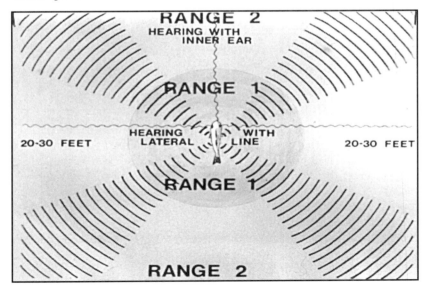

RANGE 2
HEARING WITH
INNER EAR

RANGE 1

HEARING WITH
LATERAL LINE

20-30 FEET   20-30 FEET

RANGE 1

RANGE 2

Bass are blessed with a good sense of hearing and are extremely sensitive to a wide-range of frequencies.

Jigs with built-in sound chambers like this Rattling Bootlegger Jig have become very popular in recent years.

heard and then felt, it is close enough for the fish to make the final decision to attack or let it go by, a decision guided solely by eyesight.

To catch a bass, you must first catch its eye. Sound and smell may cause an initial response, but vision is paramount.

As stated previously, the closer the lure comes, the more vibration and sound begin to stand out. Using vision, in combination with hearing and feeling, the bass pinpoints where and what it is. Naturally, the clearer the water, the more distinguishable it becomes.

Now you might ask, why is sound all that important? Well, first of all, only a small percentage of your casts will land next to a fish. But many of your casts will land your lure within 40 feet of a bass. For this reason, it is smart to make several casts to the same location (especially in stained to murky water and during low-light conditions).

Although all lures moving through water produce sound waves of some degree, lures that create additional sound and vibration will help a fish pinpoint the source of that sound quicker and naturally will benefit the angler in possibly getting more strikes. Keep in mind that the more active bass are, the more they will move in search of your offering. The more inactive they are, the slower your approach must be.

Although research in the vast field of sound has not been as thorough as the need dictates, there is very little doubt that sound with all its ramifications is a critical factor in the life of a bass. And it is equally critical from a fisherman's standpoint. As a fisherman, it is smart to be aware of the effects of sound and make them work for you — both in attracting bass and by avoiding those noisess that would have an adverse effect and frighten bass.

CHAPTER 5

THE BAITFISH CONNECTION

The largemouth bass is perhaps one of the most glamorous species in the fresh waters of the world today. They have a high intellect and a strong instinct for survival, but like all other animals bass have cycles through their lives that cause them to react in a particular manner.

The largemouth approaches the physical configuration of the perfect predator with broad, powerful tails, excellent vision, superb hearing — and the ability to maneuver underwater quickly and effectively.

Unlike members of the pike family or trout, the bass is built to probe and forage around logs, rocks, vegetation and other forms of protective cover. Sometimes these fish will strike their prey from ambush points; other times, they will simply cruise along suspended looking for food.

During these periods, their main diet consists of baitfish like shad — and believe it or not — minnows of this type spend the majority of their lives in open water away from the shoreline. But, from time to time, they will journey in close to the shallow shoreline.

Many anglers believe the reason baitfish are sometimes found along the shoreline is because wind currents have drifted them there. There is no truth to that. The wind doesn't blow the bait. Instead, what you are seeing is shad feeding. Shad are filter feeders. They feed on plankton that the wind blows in against the bank.

Forage is always on the move — sometimes shallow, sometimes deep; sometimes in, but most times out. I'm sure you have seen large areas out in a lake teaming with baitfish, and then all of a sudden, the surface explodes with feeding bass. Well, for the most part, the majority of this schooling and feeding activity takes place beneath the surface out of sight and unknown to the angler. Sometimes it happens within casting distance, but unless a bass chases a shad to the surface, you will never know it.

Quality depthfinding electronics will illustrate the close connection between bass and baitfish like shad.

So, you might ask: "Why worry about something you can't control?" Fortunately, you can control it — to a certain degree — provided you are willing to spend a little extra effort checking out the area that you plan to fish.

As fishermen, we know that bass are structure-oriented. In other words, they relate to key places such as points, flats, dropoffs, ledges and so on. But many times, bass are not tied to these bottom features. Instead, they are on the move looking for baitfish.

Back to the "little extra effort" that I mentioned earlier. When I move into an area and try several key spots at different depths that fail to produce a strike, I simply pull up my trolling motor, crank up my big motor and begin idling out away from the structure — while watching my LCG graph to see if I can locate the baitfish and the depth they are using. Sometimes I get lucky and locate bass feeding on them, which, of course, is what I wanted to do in the first place.

To be successful, predators like largemouth bass must select and attack one specific victim at a time. And because each fish in the school looks like every other one, it becomes nearly impossible for the bass to zero in on one individual baitfish. Obviously then, an isolated baitfish at the edge of a school makes the best target. Should the isolated shad look injured, it will stand out even more because of its irregular swimming movements.

It is important to get the lure to the correct depth where there is forage movement. Baitfish aren't going to be found everywhere, so you can bet when I find an area that has them, I'll spend lots of time fishing it.

There are several other factors that influence shad movement in addition to plankton that is moved about the lake by natural currents or wind: sudden changes in pH, temperature, water clarity, and lake turnover all have an effect on baitfish — just like they do with gamefish.

One of the lures that best takes advantage of the schooling action of shad is the Strike King Pork-O. It is a bait that has a wide range of applications. Primarily, it's designed to sink slowly and cover a lot of water at different depths. Because it looks so natural as it sinks, it often tempts strikes by appealing to the fish's feeding instinct. But even when the fish are not in a feeding mood, it can also trigger an aggressive reflex strike (meaning that a bass may strike it out of a simple impulse).

The slower you retrieve the lure, the more effective it will be. To give the bait more action, I pull it slowly (for about 1 to 2 feet) and twitch my wrist slightly, while keeping my rod tip in an upper position. Using lines with tests of 10 to 14 pounds will allow the lure to go even deeper and have better action than would heavier line weights like 17- to 20-pound tests.

Adding a small slip-shot just above the hook will enable you to cover deeper water, while improving your sensitivity (especially when wind is present).

Another productive lure that does a good job of imitating a shad is the Bomber Fat Free Shad, which I helped design. It works especially well in windy conditions and when the shad are 12 feet or deeper.

Keep in mind that regardless of the lure, the rod or line weight you're using, presentation is very critical. I believe that throughout the year, 90 percent of the quality bass that I'm lucky enough to catch, strike when they are offered a slow and erratic presentation.

Getting back to the characteristics of the shad population, in Chapter 2 we discussed the reasons why these baitfish bunch up so tightly. But it deserves repeating again because fishermen need to make this connection. This tight pod of shad works a couple of ways to provide some much-needed defense for the otherwise defenseless baitfish. It's the only way they can survive.

First, swimming close together gives the school an image of something much larger than just hundreds of tiny fish. This gives them the profile of a big fish, a predator of some sort. Even their

Big-bladed spinnerbaits create a vibration similar to the sound impulse of a large baitfish.

collective movement creates impulse sounds that are similar to those of a larger fish. This may fool hungry bass some of the time, but it can also be their downfall. That's because of the collective odor that all of the baitfish emit into the water. This can be detected by the largemouth's keen sense of smell and allows them to zero in on the baitfish pod like kamakaze pilots.

Often, you can locate submerged schools of baitfish by spotting the oil slick from their natural discharge as it rises to the surface. Obviously, it's very important to stay observant.

It's also possible to spot baitfish with polarized glasses. Look for dark areas below the surface and keep a keen eye out for single baitfish breaking the surface. This can be a dead giveaway to a school below. When the shad are deeper, your liquid-crystal depth-finder can pinpoint the location, the depth, and the direction they are moving.

Another important consideration is boat position. It is smart to first work the outer edges of the school before running your lure under or through them. Normally, the bass will position themselves down-wind from the baitfish because this makes them a lot easier to follow. In such cases, your casts should be made into the wind. That way, if you get a strike and hang a bass, you won't pull the fighting fish back through the school and spook it away.

Remember that a bass will usually attack an individual shad rather than attempting to catch one at random by crashing through the center of the school. This is a key point in understanding the feeding habits of predatory fish. Predators select and attack one specific victim at a time and choose a victim that is either isolated, disabled, or unique looking.

In closing, I should remind you that much of the feeding action we have been discussing — bass feeding on baitfish— takes place below the surface and out of view, normally in open water. To find and catch these fish on a fairly consistent basis, try using some of the techniques we've discussed. I think you will be pleasantly surprised at the results.

A catch like this one will leave a youngster brimming with confidence. We should all learn something from this kind of youthful exuberance.

CHAPTER 6

SEVEN KEYS TO CATCHING LARGEMOUTHS

Fooling fish is an art in itself, but tricking them into hitting something that's artificial, something that's an impostor, is really kind of special. This alone is a major part of what we call bass fishing.

To be successful at this sport involves the process of elimination. This requires a systematic approach, based on trial and error until you uncover what will produce at a given moment. Let me tell you, if a bait is worth tying on, it should be given a fair chance to produce.

Having doubt as you pull the knot tight, or even thinking of another lure that you should be using before the one you just tied on gets wet, or changing the lure only after a cast or two, are all signs of desperation and a lack of confidence — not only in the lure, but in your approach as well.

Before you switch, give it a fair shot and try to have confidence in that first lure of the day. Concentrate on the lure, how it works, on your presentation and where you are fishing it. And then use it until you are really convinced it's not going to produce at that time.

Bass lures come in all shapes and sizes and using them involves countless variables. Experience is a tremendous teacher, but only if you mentally record your wins and defeats. In the meantime, there are seven key and essential elements of bass fishing that every angler should commit to memory.

They are approach, depth, presentation, experiment, concentration, learning, and confidence. If you practice them every time you are on the water — and practice them with a lot of motivation and desire — I'll guarantee you that you will master the artificial lure game, quicker than a minnow can jump a dipper.

A guy told me recently that most fishing lures were made to catch fishermen, not fish. Surprisingly, some fishermen believe that 70 percent of the lures on the market today are made to catch the angler more so than the fish. As someone who has been in the fishing industry for a long time, I can tell you that's hog-wash. What these folks are overlooking is the time, effort, and money it takes to design a bass lure — to test it, then set up the tooling (which isn't cheap). Then comes the manufacturing and marketing of the product in hopes that it will be accepted by fishermen and will sell well. These costs are staggering, and you can bet that before a lure designer gets past the prototype stage he has already convinced and proven to himself and others that his creation will catch fish.

It's a well-known fact that some lures seem to work better than others and will catch more fish at times. And it is not uncommon to find one angler who swears by a certain bait, and another avid angler who complains that he can't catch a cold using it.

Regardless of what lure you're fishing with, it is very important to put some thought behind your cast. If the spot looks good, don't make a single cast and leave. Make several casts and psych yourself up to believe a fish is there. This will accomplish two important things. For one, you will be fishing the spot more carefully. And secondly, you will fish it much more thoroughly.

Another key component I've learned about artificial plugs is that when a bass (especially a large bass) is attracted to most lures, many times it will swim up to the bait, maybe look at it (if it is stationary) or follow it a short distance if it is moving — and then decide whether or not to bust it. If the lure doesn't suddenly change speed, action or direction — as living prey would — there is a good chance that the fish will reject it. This is why on the retrieve, you should be very conscious of your presentation changing the movement every few feet or so as you work it along. It is important you do this with any lure you fish, creating a natural erratic look, because that's one thing that often will entice a strike. Remember that you are fishing an imitator that is made of a foreign matter, so you must do all that is in your power to make it look like the real thing.

Think about this: live forage does not fight its way through the water. Instead, it swims or moves smoothly and easily as it cruises along. Sure, it may vary its speed somewhat — moving faster or slower and even stopping. But if danger threatens, it's sure going to do something different. Speed up, retreat, get gone, go crazy, play possum, try to hide. But most times it'll move out like a late freight.

When I think back over the years to the really big bass that I've been blessed to catch, one thing sure comes to mind. And that is lure presentation. Without question, a slow erratic retrieve has produced my biggest catches. And lures like the plastic worm, jig, spinnerbait (slow-rolled), crankbait (fished in a stop-and-go retrieve)

Learn to work the seven key elements of bass fishing and you will soon be admiring bass of this stature.

and even topwater lures (like the frog, prop-baits and minnow plugs) are usually the best producers. Bass, as a general rule, are not tailored to long pursuit. They are not going to chase and eat something that doesn't act half-way natural.

Let's spend a minute and discuss the importance of each of my seven essential elements for consistent success.

Approach. A bass that has become aware of or alarmed by your presence can be very difficult to catch (especially with an artificial lure). So your initial approach can be crucial.

The shallower the fish, the more critical your approach should be. To catch a bass, you first must get within casting range and then offer it something it will bite.

Depth. Establishing a depth pattern is the real key to fish-catching success. Your offering must be fished on the bass' depth level or close to it, in order for the fish to find it. The more inactive the bass, the more critical this can be.

Presentation. Establishing a rhythm with your retrieve is vital, because it is the rhythm in a lure that attracts bass. How you retrieve the bait determines the rhythm. Once you find the best presentation, stay with it until you feel it won't produce any longer. Then experiment with different retrieves until you either establish a new one or have to change baits.

Experiment. If one doesn't add this word to his fishing vocabulary and learn to practice it, he is going to find himself having lots of fishless days. When all else fails, it's the smart angler who experiments until he finds the right combination that works at that particular time.

Concentration. Fishermen who score fairly consistently depend heavily on this word. Total concentration is a major part of every move a good angler makes. He has a mental picture of the underwater terrain he's fishing and every movement of his lure and monitors each variation. Successful fishermen are always thinking and can easily duplicate any lure action that brings a strike.

Learning. This, too, is a key word. Always make it a practice to try and learn something new on every outing. You will learn a lot by observing and asking lots of questions. Remember this phrase — to learn to fish, you must fish to learn.

Confidence. This word called confidence is, without a doubt, the greatest single lure in your tackle box. The biggest factor in artificial lure fishing remains confidence in the bait you are using. Confidence can't be bought in a sporting goods store or even ac-quired from a successful, or experienced angler.

It is primarily earned through your own experience. You'll never learn everything there is to know about lure fishing. You acquire confidence through learning, experimenting and developing an understanding of the habits and habitat of your quarry. And by mastering the personalities of your tackle and finally, by slowly putting together the pieces of the fishing jigsaw puzzle.

In this chapter, we haven't discussed size, weight, and color when it comes to bass lures. These also can make a big difference, but regardless of what artificial bait you select, take the time to learn to work it as well as you can. You will discover in time that you will catch more bass on a lure that you know how to work and have confidence in.

CHAPTER 7

THE PRESENTATION GAME

Bass anglers who catch bass on a regular basis are those that believe strongly in lure presentation in order to entice the fish to eat it. Speed, depth control, lure selection, color and size, as well as placement of your cast are essential to catching bass.

Eliminating any of these factors can result in having an unsuccessful day. Often a fisherman selects the correct lure, weight and color, works it at the proper depth with the correct presentation, but fails to fish it in the right location. And there are those who do everything right, except fish the lure at the proper depth, and on it goes. To really be successful, most times you must experiment with your lure selection, the color and size, the depth and location and the speed in which you retrieve or work it.

All of this is part of the bass fishing game, and it's what makes fishing so special — trying to figure them out and lure them into hitting an artificial offering. Now that's fun!

However, there are going to be those times when, regardless of what you do, you are not going to catch them.

Let's say we've got a pretty day for fishing. The water is clear with a surface temperature of 75 degrees. We're in an area of the lake that has a good population of bass in it, along with lots of cover with good structure at different depths. Yet, with all of this, we've got one major problem, inactive bass.

So with that, what do we do? First, we must select a lure that we can work extremely slow, one that looks and acts very natural, and one we can fish over, in, through, and around the submerged cover in this area, and we must psych ourselves to work the entire area very carefully and very thoroughly even if it takes making several casts to the same spot.

The lure we've selected to use for this situation is one of the best for conditions like this — the old reliable plastic worm. I would

Lure presentation is probably the most crucial aspect of bass fishing.

probably select a Riverside Air Worm, which has better flotation than any worm I've ever seen. It will float with a 3/0 hook in it.

In the situation we're creating, we are not going to use it on top. Instead, let's team it with a light slip sinker. This way we could fish it on the bottom where it will still float up high and give the bass an opportunity to see it from a greater distance. This alone is a major plus with inactive bass.

The weight of the slip-sinker we're using is important, too. It weighs 3/16 of an ounce and gives the worm a slower, more natural fall, which can be very critical to non-aggressive bass. A sinker that is too heavy allows the worm to fall too fast, making it very unattractive.

What makes a worm so attractive to a bass? I think the fact that it represents something in the food chain. It looks, feels and acts natural. It can be fished almost anywhere, at any depth and it maintains an exact contour depth (following the bottom terrain and cover).

It's a mighty productive lure, and probably catches more fish for more people than any other lure throughout the warm-water seasons.

Speaking of how effective the worm can be, here's something you might find interesting. About 30 years ago, a southern legislator introduced a bill to outlaw the plastic worm in his state. This lure had been around for a few years before the state senator took action, but it was proving to be so deadly on bass that one man, at least, feared for the continued existence of the bass. Luckily for us, the bill failed to pass and, not surprisingly, bass still abound in southern waters.

I think that we would all agree on the fact that the last thing between you and the fish is the hook. And if you are having problems missing bass on the hook you are using, consider going to Eagle Claw's L744 Featherlite Automatic Rotating offset hook for bass.

With conventional cam-type hooks, the point is parallel to the rest of the hook. So the point follows the shaft and through the worm and many times does not hook the fish. But with the automatic rotating hook, the point rotates away from the bait and into the fish's mouth. This hook is available in half-sizes, which means that you can precisely accommodate different shapes (and thicknesses) of plastic worms.

There is no doubt about it, during these off-feed periods you have to anger a bass into striking. It is certainly not hungry. Provoking the fish into a striking mood isn't a tactic easily mastered. You have to annoy these turned-off fish into striking. You need to aggravate the bass so much that it will strike your bait not to eat, but just to eliminate the intrusion. A high-speed lure will not normally provoke an attack. A lure that closely resembles forage does well showing off its stuff and this is why a worm can be so effective. But you've got to be patient and fish it with the correct presentation and that's slow.

Timely Tactics

CHAPTER 8

MAKING CONTACT

My good friend and outdoor writer, Don Wirth of Nashville, once wrote that the concept of a contact lure is one that many bass fishermen fail to grasp. In essence, what Don is saying is that contact lures are lures that come into contact with objects, such as stumps, rocks, brush, grass or the bottom; mud, sand, gravel, clay or whatever.

The most familiar contact lures are plastic worms and jigs. And guess what lures catch the most big fish? You've got it — plastic worms and jigs. Let's analyze this for a second and learn a little more about just what turns a big bass on.

When you think about it, plastic worms and the jig-and-pork combination have little built-in action of their own. When they bump, jump or wiggle, it's because the angler made it happen or because the lure has come into contact with something.

Let's say you're fishing a jig-and-pork combo across a slick bottom. The lure will move along, kicking up little clouds of silt. Then let's say it comes into contact with a stump. Its action changes. Perhaps it hangs up momentarily, so that you have to tighten down on the bait. Then suddenly it springs off the stump. That's when a bass usually blasts it. Any experienced fisherman will tell you he's had this happen.

A jig-and-pork being reeled through the water has virtually no built-in action. It is totally up to the fisherman — and the object with which the bait comes into contact — to create the action.

Considering this concept even more, you realize that some lures have a mechanical action. Lures with random action are inevitably contact lures. Random action is caused when the lure bumps into something and changes its speed or angle or profile. Live baitfish have random action. You won't see a minnow, shad or other swimming forage swim 100 feet without speeding up, slowing down, turning, darting and so on. Bass know that food that is safe to eat has a random action which looks and acts natural.

Crankbaits, on the other hand, have built-in action. The design of the lure, the length, or angle of its diving lip, its weight and several other factors all contribute to its particular action. The problem with crankbaits, though, is that most fishermen depend on their mechanical or built-in action to catch fish.

True, you can have a fine day catching small bass by smoking a crankbait. But for big bass, it's smart to think of a crankbait as a contact lure.

When you cause your crankbait to come into contact with an object, you change its action from mechanical to random. The lure may wiggle along through open water and then suddenly hit a bush, stump or whatever and then veer off to one side. Invariably, this is when the strike will occur.

"Sure it will," you may say, "because there was a bass sitting next to the object." But this isn't always the case. Many times, I've seen bass follow a crankbait in open water without striking, then suddenly attack the lure when it changes direction after hitting something. That sudden, random action, the same random action that live food exhibits, triggers a strike.

Many beginning bass anglers are somewhat afraid of casting their expensive lure too close to cover, but like the old saying goes; you aren't fishing, if you aren't hanging.

To create a random action with a crankbait where no cover is present, it's smart for the angler to create an erratic action as he reels the lure in. Vary the speed from fast to slow, from slow to stop and from stop to fast until you find the best presentation for that given time and situation.

Crankbaits are excellent lures for covering lots of water quickly and they are the type of bait you can easily find submerged objects with.

There is really no question why some bass anglers are more consistent than others. Those who catch the majority of fish do one very important thing — they zero in on where the bass live.

It's a known fact that bass, especially largemouths, rely heavily on structure and cover more than most other gamefish. That structure is the geologic makeup of the lake floor, regardless if it's man-made or natural. Ichthyologists like Dr. Loren Hill, have proven this fact in simple, controlled experiments. Dr. Hill placed several bass in a white-sided tank in which the light was evenly distributed and where no sounds could be heard. The bass swam about as if they were lost. Then he placed some cover on one side of the tank and the fish immediately moved to the cover. From the moment they are born, bass instinctively relate to cover.

Bringing a lure into contact with an object gives it an enticing, erratic action.

At first, it is to avoid being eaten by other fish and birds. As they mature, they become the dominant predator and select cover such as stumps, bushes, logs, vegetation, and boulders as ambush points to feed on a wide assortment of unsuspecting prey.

Because the life of a bass revolves around structure and available cover, fishermen who become adept at locating different forms of underwater terrain invariably catch more fish.

The more we learn about how these super creatures relate to structure and cover in our lakes and rivers, the more consistent we will become at winning the match with them.

Now you might ask, how do you find submerged structure and cover? Well, first let me say that the key is to find structure with cover, and the best way to go about this is to use a good map to show you where the key structural features are. Then a good liquid-crystal depthfinder (my choice is Eagle's Ultra III Plus) will help you find it, show if cover is present and at what depth. This takes time, concentration and work, but it's the type of work that offers great rewards if you're the kind of guy who's willing to exert some effort. Finding good places can pay off for a long time to come. Believe it or not, I know some fishing holes that still produce for me today just as well as they did twenty years ago. And surprisingly most of the original cover is still there. Sure, they took some time and effort to find, but boy, it was really worth it!

Let's define the exact meaning of the word **structure**.

Consider structure to be the floor of the lake extending from the shallows to the deeper water. But more precisely, it is the unusual or irregular features on the lake bottom that are different from the surrounding bottom areas. A stump tipped on its side in a foot or two of water along the shoreline is structure. And a creek bed meandering along the bottom of a lake at a depth of 25 feet is also structure.

Structure comes in all sizes and shapes. It can be straight or crooked, contain dents and depressions, or be flat. Some structure is long, some is short. Some is steep, sloping, barren, brushy, grassy, stumpy, rocky or mossy. It can be shallow or deep — on the shore-line or offshore in open water.

One of the best ways to grasp the concept of structure is to use your imagination when you're driving along a highway. Look at the surrounding countryside and picture what it would look like if the entire area were suddenly inundated with water. Start trying to pick the places where bass would be most likely to hang out. You might start with the drainage ditch alongside the road you're driving on and around the culvert you just crossed.

As you go through these mental gyrations, you will start to associate stands of trees along the field perimeters as a specific type of structure. Some fields will slope and others will be flat with perhaps a drop-off on one side. The idea is to be able to visualize what your favorite lake might look like if the water were suddenly drawn down. Many anglers find it difficult to picture the physical features of a lake bottom once it is covered with water. You may know that there is a roadbed or ditch below the surface, but unless you train yourself you don't always visualize it when you are fishing.

As I said earlier, a map and depthfinder can help you gain the necessary mental picture. But if you also associate features with those you can see above the ground, it becomes a lot easier. Then, the next time you fish a creek bed shouldering into a point you might be able to compare it to one you've seen on the way to the lake.

It is important to remember that every key spot you locate will not hold fish, but such places should never be forgotten and should be checked again periodically. It could be that the fish weren't there when you were, or maybe the spot just happens to be at the wrong depth at that given time. Make a mental note of it and go back until you are totally convinced that the fish don't use it.

There is simply no doubt about it — structure is a fisherman's cornerstone for success. And if cover is there at the magical depth and you allow your lure to make contact with it, the odds are really good that you, too, will make contact.

CHAPTER 9

PORK —
THE ULTIMATE LURE

Have you ever thought about how quickly certain things become outdated? That dress or skirt you like to see your wife wear; the camera you bought last year; the computer you purchased six months ago. It's kind of special to buy a product that doesn't lose its value, usefulness or become obsolete shortly after you get it.

One such item that never seems to lose its effectiveness is the fishing lure. I've heard anglers say, "that old bait won't produce like it used to. It's too old. Bass grow leery of seeing the same old lure all the time." I disagree with that. I don't believe a bass' memory is that good. I base this on the fact that I have caught three bass in my life that had a second lure in their mouth when I hooked them. Surprisingly, what I caught these three largemouths on was an identical bait to the one that was already hooked in their mouths. Two were plastic worms and the other a 900-Series Hellbender.

Another time, I caught the same bass three times in less than a week in a farm pond, on the same bait. The reason I know it was the same fish is because it had two distinguishable black marks on its tail. It was fat, approximately 4 pounds, and a very healthy fish that wasn't starving. Plus it had two additional hook marks in its mouth.

Artificial lures that were discontinued or no longer popular can and are still highly effective in catching bass. How can a 5-pound bass be leery of a lure that was built and discontinued 20 years ago? If largemouths are so lure conscious and smart enough to recognize the same bait all of the time, why are so many caught on the jig-and-pork combination, grubs and plastic worms year after year?

I think when you cast a particular bait all day and it doesn't produce, it's because you didn't fish it properly or at the correct depth or location. Possibly the fish were inactive and wouldn't hit anything that day. I just don't believe the reason a lure doesn't produce is because the bass are tired or leery of seeing it. Fishing lures don't get old and go out of style — at least not with bass.

A prime example is one of my favorites, called the Strike King Pork-O. Its concept, look and style are older than my children. It is nothing more than a 7 1/4-inch piece of pork rind. The only thing new about it is that it has been designed and trimmed with a uniquely new cut and scented. This puts it a step above what we used 30 years ago. We caught a lot of bass then with this concept and today we're still catching bass on it. It's something old, with something kind of new in the form of a twist-and-twitch technique.

The Strike King Pork-O

The erratic action of this bait, its scent, and its flavor enhancement increases the intensity and the number of strikes from long distances. I have found it is best to slowly work the Pork-O like you would work a minnow plug like a Rapala. This bait will dart, dip, jump, twist and twitch. And this erratic motion will trigger strikes if presented properly.

It is always smart to experiment with any lure you fish and especially with this one. You should always pay special attention to the position of your rod tip. The versatility of this lure enables the angler to fish this lure successfully under a variety of conditions and depths. The key to fishing this lure most effectively is to force yourself not to overwork the bait with a lot of wrist and rod tip action. That will only spoil the natural action. When you barely twitch your rod tip, the bait will have plenty of movement, believe me. The angler who settles on a simple, slow and steady retrieve will enjoy the best results. The key is not to over-power the lure.

I have my best success by holding my rod tip in an upper position and constantly watching my line as the bait moves forward. When I feel the hit or see my line moving off, I continue a slow retrieve until the line gets fairly tight. With my rod tip pointing up to the 10 o'clock position, I then set the hook with a strong upward jerk. Be careful and not let the bass have too much time with this lure. With minimal weight a fish will think it's the real thing and swallow it quickly.

Often when there is a slight current (caused by either the wind or water being pulled) or the bass are a little deeper, you will find that adding a small split-shot just above your hook will help.

Dick Tillman with living proof of the unparalleled allure of the Pork-O.

You will have more sensitivity, as well as be able to fish the area more thoroughly.

Let me tell you something else about this lure. To me, it represents the ultimate qualities in attracting attention and triggering strikes. It is without question the next best thing to live bait. That is a mighty strong statement, but I honestly believe that.

Let me tell you why.

First, it displays virtually no negative cues to the bass. It has a random action as you work it, rather than a mechanical motion. It looks and feels very natural and makes no noise. It's long and thin in shape, meaning it has an excellent profile. It bears a strong resemblance to living prey. Its appearance and look resembles a variety of natural foods. Because it presents very few negative cues, it is hard for a bass to reject it.

Let me tell you several other key reasons why this bait is so effective. It's made from pork, which is a fantastic, versatile product that can be used on a lure like a jig or by itself as we've been discussing. Pork has great natural action — much more than plastic. It has a natural texture and this pork, manufactured by Strike King, contains salt. A salty flavor that definitely tastes like something alive tells the bass that it is food (which is why a largemouth will hold on to it considerably longer than other artificial lures).

Earlier I mentioned two words about this lure. One of these words was its attracting qualities and the other was triggering qualities. Attracting qualities are those aspects of a lure that capture the bass' attention. The triggering qualities are the characteristics of a lure that cause the fish to make a commitment and hit it. Every artificial lure must have a few attracting and triggering qualities if it is going to catch bass. It is worthless if a lure has attracting qualities to prick a bass' attention, but not enough of a triggering mechanism to elicit a strike. A triggering quality alone isn't enough, but a fish will likely not notice the lure unless it was directly in front of its nose.

This is the type of lure is used in either clear or shallow stained water. It's an eye contact lure, meaning it has no or very little vibration and a largemouth needs to see it to be able to hit it.

This lure's ability to mimic real life is absolutely remarkable. The Pork-O is something old with something new — and something for all bass enthusiasts.

CHAPTER 10

LURES THAT DO ME PROUD

I can honestly say that I have never caught a bass I didn't like. However, I have caught some I liked more than others. And you know it has more meaning when you can trick them into biting something that's artificial.

Have you ever wondered what makes a bass hit these things? Well, there are many factors that entice a bass to strike a lure at a particular time.

One would be color. A fish has got to be able to see it to eat it. Another would be size and shape. It has to be the proper size and shape for the fish to think he can swallow it.

Action would certainly have to be a major factor. It must be attractive enough with the proper moves to attract their attention. Vibration would be another, especially in a murky to muddy water environment. A bass that lives in these conditions needs to hear it to find it and, of course, odor would also have to be considered many times.

From the anglers standpoint, there are factors he must consider: water clarity, water temperature, depth, type of terrain, type of cover, time of year, type of equipment, lure selection and presentation.

I'd like to share with you some helpful hints and tips about fishing several of my most productive lures. I will be discussing some of the when, where, and how's of fishing spinnerbaits, buzzbaits, jigs, crankbaits, plastic worms and pork baits.

A few minutes ago, I said the word "equipment." So let's first start with it. Of the lures I just mentioned my No. 1 choice in tackle is a baitcasting outfit. That's simply because I have the most confidence in fishing larger lures and can handle them much easier with this as opposed to spinning tackle. Now I'm not saying I don't enjoy spinning gear, because I do. But water clarity, type of cover, and size of lure will usually dictate my choices. However, if I've got a choice, it would be baitcasting — simply because of the power it offers and its ability to handle heavier line weight. It provides tremendous strength and power. And we know that bass are the type of fish that prefers cover — the thicker the better.

In my opinion, the most versatile bass fishing lure on the market today is the **spinnerbait**. Why is it classified as the most versatile? Simply because it can be fished summer, fall, winter and spring. In hot water, cold water, muddy water and clear water; from just under the surface to as deep as you want to fish it. It is also the type of lure that can be fished in, over, through and around many forms of cover. Spinnerbaits come in single-blade and tandem-blade models. Single blades produce the strongest beat and are ideal for free falling and bottom bouncing (making them an excellent all around choice).

Tandem models have more water resistance so they run shallower at a given retrieve speed and are very effective for waking the surface and producing more flash.

Here are some of my most productive spinnerbait tips:

√ For more vibration, select a single blade.

√ For more flash, select tandem blades.

√ For vegetation, use willowleaf blades.

√ For less wind resistance and more action, use lifelike Mirage silicone skirts instead of vinyl.

√ During low-light conditions and in heavily stained water, select single blades for more vibration.

√ Whenever you detect a pause in the beat of a blade, set the hook.

√ In cold water, use blades that create the most water resistance, which allows for a slower presentation.

√ Use a pork attractor (trailer) for more appeal, more buoyancy and greater lift.

√ Add a trailer hook for combating short strikes.

√ If the terrain will permit, reverse the trailer hook for an even better strike-catch ratio.

√ Experiment with different retrieves, sizes and colors.

√ Select and fish a spinnerbait that offers the most reflection and vibration for best results.

Now, let's discuss another one of my favorite lures — **deep diving crankbaits**.

One of the greatest advantages of fishing with lures of this type is the vast amount of water you can cover with them, especially when bass are using a depth of 10-20 feet. The versatility of crank-

The plastic worm probably catches more largemouths than any other lure every year. This big Florida trophy is proof.

baits are really limited only by the imagination and cleverness of the user. Crankbaits (like my favorite — Bomber's Fat Free Shad) require the correct presentation, the proper speed and precise depth control. All are vital to success.

Here are some tips that will surely improve your success when fishing crankbaits:

√ For maximum depth control without modification, use a moderate to slow retrieve.

√ For best bass appeal, use an erratic retrieve.

√ For best lure performance tie directly to the O-ring on the lure.

√ For additional depth, add a 1/4- to 3/8-ounce slip sinker.

√ For more vibration and sound, use crankbaits with internal rattles.

√ To help eliminate hang-ups, remove the front outside hook.

√ If the lure runs to the right, bend the line tie to the left (and vice-versa is it is running off to the left).

√ For better depth control, use a lighter weight line. But not too light — 10-pound test or higher.

√ Concentrate on speed and depth control.

The next highly productive lure I'd like to discuss is the **jig-and-pork** combination.

Jigs have been catching bass for years and still are perhaps one of the most productive baits on the market today (especially in water clarity ranging from slightly murky to clear; in water temperature below the 65 degree range; and when bass are in an inactive mood and buried up in those tight-cover areas). Jigs are presentation lures and the key to fishing them is to make them look as much alive as possible. That is created with a slow presentation, and by adding pork to them.

A pork trailer extends the bait, creating a larger image that is the more attractive and adds more action for appeal and buoyancy for a slower fall on the retrieve. In fishing this lure, cast it out and let it settle to the bottom. Then begin a slow jigging-type retrieve, working the rod tip from the 10 o'clock to 12 o'clock position. Let the rod tip add the natural light action to the lure. As the jig settles to the bottom, repeat the same motion again and again.

Here are some additional tips on fishing these fantastic lures:

√ Keep a supply of different weight jigs, ranging from 3/16- to 3/4-ounce, for different water temperatures, clarity and types of cover.

√ Select jigs with a strong, sharp hook, as well as a built-in rattle.

√ Jig fishing demands a lot of concentration.

√ To improve your feel and maintain your maximum pounds of hooksetting power, use a fast-action rod between 6 and 6 1/2 feet in length.

√ Keep your hooks sharp. Sharp hooks penetrate more easily and are harder to dislodge.

√ Fish jigs slowly during all seasons — but extremely slow in cold water.

√ Check your line and knot periodically.

√ Pay close attention to jig colors.

√ Learn the importance of jig sizes and how to fish each size.

√ Stay alert, have patience, be motivated and think positively.

The next type of lures that make me proud is a noisy, bubbling, churning thing called the **buzzbait**.

The buzzbait is classified as a topwater lure, but it differs from other surface plugs because it is constantly moving. It produces best from mid-spring to mid-fall, when the water temperature ranges from 65 degrees and above. It can be fished in, through, around and over many forms of cover due to its shape and design. It also produces best with a slow erratic presentation.

As anglers, we know that a slow-moving lure gives the predator more time to locate and zero in on the bait. The key in buzzbait fishing is to put some thought behind each cast. If the spot looks good, don't make a cast and leave. Instead, make several casts and psych yourself up to believe a bass is there. When you do this, you will accomplish two things — you will fish the area more carefully and, secondly, more thoroughly.

Here are some good buzzbait tips:

√ For better lure and line control, as well as better hooksets, keep your rod tip up.

√ Add a frog chunk for buoyancy and lift.

√ Add a trailer hook when short strikes occur (provided the cover will allow it.)

√ Change retrieve speeds often. This will cause the lure to produce an erratic, inviting baitfish sound.

√ To improve your strike-catch ratio, set the hook by feel, rather than by sight or sound.

√ Increase your odds by making several casts to the same area.

We discussed the Strike King **Pork-O** in the last chapter, but I cannot leave it out of a list of the Lures That Do Me Proud.

It's a lure that you will really enjoy using — and not just because it catches fish. It is also just plain fun to fish. It is the kind of

**My friend Bill Wolbrecht shows off a big Arkansas bass that fell
victim to a Riverside Big Wag worm.**

lure that can be fished almost anywhere (on, over, around and even
through most forms of cover) and even in open water. Another super
feature about this exciting bait is that it allows you the opportunity to
get a strike that you would never have otherwise gotten. And it gives
you the opportunity to catch fish simply because it can be fished
effectively in thick places.

Here are a few tips for specialty lures like the Pork-O:

√ Lures of this type should be fished slowly, enabling
neighboring bass to make ample eye contact with it. Also, a slow
retrieve provides a better action.

√ When fishing vegetation (high-percentage bass areas), target the points, pockets, holes, dips, cuts and any other irregular feature.

√ Always be observant, have patience and concentrate on your presentation.

√ Fast-action 6-foot rods and longer are best, because they allow for better line and lure control. And these rods help tremendously in obtaining a powerful hookset and control over a big largemouth.

√ Use a heavy line. This will eliminate stretch, provide more strength and be less abrasive.

√ Be aware of boat position. It is not uncommon in and around cover areas for a bass to follow the action above and blast the lure as soon as it clears the cover and enters open water. If you are too close, you will spook that catchable fish.

√ Concentrate on fishing cover close to deeper water.

√ Strike a fish by feel, rather than sight.

√ Check your knot and hook (for sharpness) periodically.

Another very popular lure that probably catches more largemouths for more people more consistently than any other lure on the American market is the **plastic worm**. And I am a fan of the Riverside Big Wag worm that has an incredible action.

Throughout the warm water seasons — when the water temperature is above 60 degrees — the plastic worm is one of the most consistent bass-producers available today. The worm is an eye-contact bait, meaning a fish must see it to hit it. Therefore, it produces best in a clear water environment. What makes it such a high-percentage offering is that it feels and looks natural, can be fished at all visible depths and through most forms of cover.

Here are some tips that will improve your worm fishing:

√ Match the size of the hook to the head diameter of the worm. Example: a 3/0 to 4/0 hook is ideal for most 7- to 8-inch worms. A 1/0 hook is too small, while a big 6/0 version is way too big.

√ Use the lightest slip sinker you can. The lighter the weight, the more natural action the worm will have.

√ To increase your strike-catch ratio by more than 50 percent, use a wide-gap worm hook (like Eagle Claw's round-bend, light-wire Featherlite L700 or L744 hooks that comes in half-sizes).

√ Never allow a bass to swim with the worm. On the strike, take up the excess slack and set the hook as quickly as possible.

√ Be conscious of hook sharpness.

√ For more sensitivity and better hooksets, use a fast-action rod with plenty of backbone.

√ Always set the hook with a strong upward jerk.

√ Worm fishing places a premium on concentration.

√ Allow the rod tip to work the rod from 10 o'clock to 12 o'clock. As the worm settles back to the bottom, repeat this motion over again until you have covered the area.

√ Color makes a big difference. So it is important to have a good assortment of different worm colors, length and bullet weights.

√ Be a line watcher. Stay alert for any twitch or any side movement of the line.

In this chapter, I hope I have cast enough tips your way to make you aware that lure fishing involves countless variables. But if you practice some of them enthusiastically, it won't be long before you master the artificial lure game.

CHAPTER 11

THE THRILL OF TOPWATERS

I'd like to share with you one of the most exciting ways I know to catch bass, and that's on top. There is a unique challenge to topwater fishing — and there isn't a bass angler I know that doesn't get a lump in his or her throat from a bass as it wakes the surface and blasts a surface bait.

This method of fishing is an excellent way to introduce a beginner to the sport, simply because they can see what's going on. And there's no mistaking the results of their efforts.

A high percentage of the strikes you get are not little delicate ticks or a loss of feeling in the lure. They are honest-to-goodness, breath-taking, heart-pounding, knee-bending, wide-eyed, nerve-shattering moments that rank a full 10 when it comes to real excitement.

There is no doubt about it — a tremendous amount of excitement comes from being able to see a bass strike. But that can create problems in topwater fishing, particularly when it comes to setting the hook. When the water explodes around your lure, the tendency is to bust him immediately. But when you do, you are going to miss catchable bass. You will have much better success by striking a fish by feel, rather than by sight or sound. This can be one of the hardest things in the world to master, but if you pause that extra second or two (while keeping a semi-tight line) and wait until you feel the fish, you will significantly improve your strike-catch ratio.

Timing is very important. Keep your rod tip up, be patient, grit your teeth and you will be the one that comes out on top.

With surface plugs, there is a tendency among bass fishermen to set a hook by rearing back and jerking the living fire out of the rod. This hard hookset is good, but it seldom does the job. The best hookset is to keep the rod in front of you and, after the initial hookset, set it several more times with short, sharp upward jerks.

Your rod doesn't have to move through a very wide arc to accomplish this.

Before you set the hook on any fish, the line between the rod tip and the fish must be semi-tight. Slack line prevents the action of the rod from being transmitted to the hook.

Any strike on an artificial plug is a direct take — that is, the bass intends to swallow it directly. You can be sure the fish isn't about to hold the plug in its mouth, play with it, and then swallow it.

Heddon's three-hook Zara Spook

I know, however, there are exceptions like when you are using soft plastic lures, foam and pork baits, bass have the tendency to hold on to them for a longer period. But it is an entirely different situation with hard lures. No way. Bass quickly realize that it is not the real thing and immediately try to spit it out. Yet, this takes longer to happen than you might suspect.

When a bass opens his mouth to hit any bait or lure, it also swallows water. In fact, the bait really floats into the fish's mouth and continues to float while the excess water is being expelled through the gills. Usually, a fish won't detect an artificial lure until it has ejected the water and clamps down on it.

Like I said earlier, the major mistake among fishermen using artificial baits is to set the hook too quick. Now, don't misunderstand me and believe that you have lots of time. But you do have much more than you would suspect. So if you are missing fish that you feel you should be hooking, think about what I've said — it does work.

Rebel's Zell Rowland Super Pop-R

One of my very favorite surface lures is the Strike King Grass Frog. It is an extremely exciting and fun bait to fish. It's the type of lure that I classify as a specialty lure. A specialty lure is a type of bait that was designed primarily to be fished successfully any time bass are located in shallow water. But there is a specific time and place when lures of this type are the only type of bait that you can use. When fishing in, over, through, and around thick vegetation such as lily pads, smart weed, pepper grass, penny wart, milfoil, hydrilla, eel grass, coontail (as well as thick log jams, brush and even brushy tree tops), these lures are a must. And the frog is the type of specialty lure that will enable you to get a strike that you would not have otherwise gotten — simply because no other type bait can be worked where this bait can.

This bait is made of a very durable lifelike foam. It has one big hook, which rides in a weedless position behind the bait. And when the strike occurs, the foam is compressed and the hook pushes up in prime position to penetrate. Attached to the main hook is a cheater (or trailer) hook, which definitely will increase your strike-catch ratio by almost 90 percent.

Most lures like this are classified as a 50/50 strike-catch ratio lure. If you get 10 strikes on them you are lucky if you catch five fish out of those 10 strikes. By adding this little trailer hook, you will increase those odds to 80 to 90 percent. And what is so surprising, is that this little trailer hook is almost completely weedless.

The Grass Frog is the type of lure that should be fished as slowly as possible. Whether you are fishing it over vegetation or in open-water areas, this enables the bass to make ample eye or sound contact with the lure. A fast presentation is a no-no. Frogs don't move at 40 or 50 miles per hour across the surface of the water, so it is important that you make it look as natural as you possibly can. The leg action on this frog helps it to look very natural, but only if it is worked in a natural manner. When working a lure of this type, it's important to remember to create different retrieves. By doing this you'll create an erratic cripple sound.

This lure may look large, and that's good, simply because there is more room for contact and less margin for error. It creates a larger image, which can be seen much easier, and it creates more sound as it moves. If the lure appears to be live forage, bass will — when given a choice — blast the biggest mouthful possible, (especially during the warm water season when their metabolism is increased). To entice more strikes on a bait of this type, it should sound and appear vulnerable, as well as edible. The action should suggest that the creature is in trouble. An injured, unaware forage will convince a bass to eat it.

As I said earlier, bass seldom pay attention to prey that runs the 100-yard dash in 10 seconds. If it shoots by quickly out of their strike range, they will normally pass it up (especially big fish).

When this bait was first designed, it was truly designed for fishing those hard-to-get-to places such as vegetation and some of the other visible objects we discussed. But in testing the bait, I found that this particular lure has tremendous eye appeal and it would call up fish in open water areas like you wouldn't believe The reason for this is because it looks so natural and it sends off a natural sound as it

Imitation frogs like the Grass Frog are perfect for swimming in, over, through and around thick, shallow vegetation.

plops on the surface. This alone can attract attention. Don't believe that a frog moving across the surface won't send off significant sound waves, because it does. It is perhaps a much more attractive sound than other lures. Lures of this type are calling baits. Often times unnatural sounds —or unfamiliar sounds — will spook fish. Bass are especially aware of sounds that are part of their environment and sensitive to all sounds in their environment.

So, offering something that looks, feels, and sounds natural gives you a much better chance.

For more sound, try Strike King's new Pop'N Grass Frog.

Some days topwater fishing will be as hot and fast as a bullfrog on July asphalt, while other days it won't. But if fish it during the prime seasons from mid-spring to early-fall, you can usually catch at least a few bass. So if you want to add something really special to your fishing, try a Grass Frog and don't count on winning every trip. Instead, enjoy the greatest bassing excitement you've ever known. It truly is the biggest thrill of bass fishing.

CHAPTER 12

THE VERSATILE CAROLINA-RIG

It's a known fact that the more bass we can put a lure in front of, the better our chances are of having a successful day of fishing. In order to do that, we must fish the type of lure that can cover lots of water quickly. For shallow-water fishing from 1 to 3 feet, a spinnerbait is a good choice. For mid-depth ranges, say from 4 to 10 feet, a crankbait is the answer. But for deeper depths (10 to 30 feet), a Carolina rig is one of the most efficient ways to fish deep becaus you can use casting or spinning gear with it. You can use different size lines, depending on the terrain. It is weedless, so you can fish it in grass, along ledges, around stumps and on a clean bottom. Best of all, it's easy and fun to use.

It's one of the best deeper water fish-finding techniques we have available to us as fishermen.

The Carolina rig is one of bass fishing's oldest and most effective fishing techniques. Although this heavy lead, swivel and leader technique has been in use since the early 50's, it later declined in popularity as the style of bass fishing changed over the years. But today, it's strong again, perhaps one of the hottest techniques in bass fishing.

In this chapter, I'm going to share with you some tips on how I rig it and where I'm fishing it.

But first, I think it's only fair to mention that I would never say the Carolina rig is a better or a worse rig than the Texas rig. Both have their place. A Carolina rig isn't a replacement for the Texas rig; it's just a complement to it. Fishermen who have learned how versatile it can be will add a productive, new dimension to their fishing.

For years, anglers used a plastic worm on this rig and today many still do. But others are modifying the Carolina rig to suit existing water and structure conditions. You don't have to use a plastic worm at all; in fact, many fishermen don't. Many, including

A Carolina-rigged Big Foot Lizard helped Jim Bitter win a 1995 B.A.S.S. event on Minnesota's Lake Minnetonka.

me, are using pork and let me tell you why. Pork, in my opinion, has several advantages over plastic. It looks so alive in the water. It has an unmatched texture, taste and feel. Because of its appearance and looks, it surely does resemble a variety of natural foods. It presents

very few negative cues. Plus, it is virtually in
You can use it again and again.

Two of my favorites for Carolina-rig
Carolina Liz and Bo-Leech. Made of pork, b
buoyancy and all the action you could ever ¿
the leg-kicking action when you pull it throi

I rig it on a weedless 3/0 Lightn'in ℥
especially designed for it. This pork is sprinkicu ⸳⸳⸳
for reflection, making it an ideal lure for this particular technique.

The lure and hook are on a leader that is approximately 18 to
20 inches in length and tied to one end of the swivel to prevent line
twist. Attached to the other end of the swivel is the main line that
goes to the reel. On the main line, I use a 3/4 oz sinker, and in front
of that I thread on a bead. The plastic bead serves two important
functions. One, it helps cushion the knot from wear caused by the
heavy sinker. And secondly, the bead adds the important element of
sound (as the sinker taps it).

I think sound is a big benefit with the Carolina rig and a
second bead can be added for more sound. A bass that has seen this
rig moving along and has decided not to whack it can sometimes
have its mind changed by a couple of good sounding clicks on the
next bait movements.

An important part of this rig is the length of the leader. I
personally prefer to use a leader around 18 to 20 inches, because I
feel I have better control of the bait with less line and rod movement.
And I can keep the bait in contact with a shorter leader and detect a
strike much easier.

The length of the leader affects how your bait performs in
cover. A short leader can get you more hits when bass are holding
tight to cover or are less active and won't move to a bait (especially
after a front and during the winter and early spring). If the bass are
active or are suspended above the cover, a 4- or 5-foot leader can
keep the bait above the cover, where the fish see it better. Leader
length can make a real difference in your catch.

Unlike the Texas rig, the Carolina rig allows the bait to hold
over the cover and gives the fish more time to react to it. The leader
also works for you as the bait falls. The Texas rig drops at a constant
speed dictated by a sinker, worm and line size combination. But the
Carolina rig falls at sinker speed until the lead hits. Then the lizard
(or other lure) does a little two-step, changes speed and continues
down with a slower, lazier action.

When you pull this rig up off the bottom, the lizard comes up
with a slower rise and has a totally different movement from the
Texas rig on the drop. That difference in presentation can often make

ce in your catch. Bass can be very temperamental, and
s it is the little things you do that make the difference in
or failure. Another advantage to the Carolina rig is that you
eep it in one small area and make it exhibit action and move-
nt far longer than you can the Texas rig. The ability to work it up
ext to cover or structure and leave it there for a while can often
draw strikes when faster retrieves fail.

It's hard to beat a pork lizard or leech when it comes to
Carolina-rigging. But a plastic lizard like Riverside's Floating Air
Lizard can be mighty effective as it rides up off of the lake bottom.
I've also caught bass consistently by Carolina-rigging a Floating Air
Worm and Air Fry.

Normally you fish this rig in open water and are not concerned about making pinpoint casting to targets. That's good because
the Carolina rig is difficult to cast especially with a long leader. To
help you with your cast, the preferred rod is a 7 to 7 1/2 foot fast
action because it makes casting and working the rig so much easier.
The longer rod allows for a better hookset (which is more of a
sweeping motion with a Carolina rig than a snap-set) and the extra
length allows you to take up a lot of line fast.

Perhaps the most popular size sinker weight is the 3/4-ounce.
The heavier weight makes casting easier and gets the lure down
much quicker. It helps for better feel — especially in current conditions or when you have a lot of water to cover in a short time.

When the strike occurs on this rig, you don't usually feel a
tap-tap. You usually feel resistance when you start forward movement of your bait. When you experience this, hold what you've got,
take up the slack and set the hook hard.

In summary, the Carolina rig isn't just a technique, it's a
complete system of fishing. And you know what's the best part of
the system — it really catches bass in a big, big way.

CHAPTER 13

LONG-DISTANCE FLIPPING

A highly productive method of bass fishing was introduced to anglers everywhere by a California fisherman named Dee Thomas during the mid-70s on Bull Shoals Lake. The method was called flipping — a system of getting a lure to those hard-to-reach places where bass bury up tight in thick cover areas. Not only did flipping allow you to present a bait where bass hide, it also ensured a softer lure presentation and better accuracy to place a jig-and-pork combination, a plastic worm or grub into a small opening around various forms of aquatic vegetation (tree tops and brush as well as other thick objects).

It wasn't long after Thomas scored the tournament win on Bull Shoals that his technique captured the imagination of serious bass fishermen across the country.

Flipping is a fairly simple art, so anglers of all skill levels should be able to master it to some degree. The result has been more and bigger bass for many fishermen, but there are some innovative fishermen who have taken the art of flipping to a few advanced stages. These anglers have set themselves apart from others with their consistent success, with a technique first called long-distance flipping.

Today, most anglers know it as "pitching."

This method of fishing is extremely productive in clear water. The extra distance helps prevent spooking catchable bass and allows you to flip-cast to 35- to 40-foot targets that you normally just can't reach by traditional flipping. This technique expands the normal range of conventional flipping from 15 to 20 feet into a comfortable range of 30 to 40 feet. And that extra 10 or 20 feet farther than the normal flip can be extremely productive many times.

This form of casting adds another dimension to flipping. Not only are you able to avoid spooking fish with quiet, accurate casts, you are able to hit so many more spots in a day's time because the cast is one continuous motion. You're not wasting time reeling it all the way back in and casting again.

Let me describe how this method is done. Put the reel on free-spool and let out a rod's length of line. Hold the lure in your free hand. Dip the rod tip toward the water and quickly snap it upward while letting go of the lure. The lure should swing forward and remain close to the surface on an nearly straight trajectory. As the lure moves forward and starts pulling line off of the reel, begin lifting the rod up to control the lure's height above the water. Even with a 30-foot cast, the lure might not get more than 3 feet high. As a result, it has a very quiet entry.

It takes practice to get good at this. It is not as accurate as regular traditional flipping because you're dealing with larger distances. No doubt about it, the flip-cast is very accurate, because you are using a pendulum motion. You are swinging the lure on a 7- or 8-foot swing coming off the rod tip. By using your hand to guide the lure instead of just letting it swing free, there is less room for error. By starting the lure off in your hand, you can kind of aim it. You can actually line it up for better accuracy.

A long rod is a major plus for this type of fishing and there are several reasons why. It helps you get big bass out of tight cover. You can move the fish farther and quicker after you hook it. You have more control over the fish. You can present your lure at a longer distance with less effort. You have better leverage and you can take more slack out of your line much quicker for a better hookset. A 6 1/2-foot rod will work, but a 7 1/2-footer is better. My favorite in this situation is the Quantum Tour Edition 7 foot Pitchin' Rod (TC 707FJ) teamed with a Quantum Pro 3C reel.

All anglers should remember that a fishing rod is simply a lever. Its advantage is not one of power, but rather speed. What this means is that fishing rods, depending on their length, expedite the energy of the hook-setting motion. Naturally, a long rod will pull the line farther with the same effort than a shorter rod — which should move the hook farther and faster. Simply stated, you will hook more bass with a long rod than with the standard 5- to 5 1/2-footer. The rod you select needs to be fairly stiff, as well. The more the rod bends under stress, the less energy is available to move the hook.

And again, my top three flipping/pitching baits are the jig-and-pork, the plastic worm and the grub.

One of the most important aspects of this method is total concentration on what you are doing and what is happening to the

Roland Martin winches a big bass from a treacherous logjam.

lure. Being a line-watcher is important — and even this doesn't always mean you will be able to detect a hit. You almost have to develop a feeling from within that tells you when a largemouth has mouthed your lure. One way to develop this awareness is to set the hook whenever in doubt. In the beginning it won't be a fish at all, but it doesn't cost anything to set the hook. Over time, there will be a

Pitching changed the sport for myself and most bass anglers.

fish on nearly every time you jerk. You will develop confidence in your senses and begin to recognize the different ways a strike can feel.

Another key to this game is boat positioning and control. With practice, you will develop a comfort range, a distance from which you will prefer to flip or pitch. You will be able to vary your distances as you develop a preferred range. Keeping your boat at this distance will allow you to have the maximum amount of control over your line and lure.

CHAPTER 14

THE JIG-AND-PIG: WHEN ALL ELSE FAILS

I believe it would be safe to say that over the past 10 years or so, no other fishing lure has had the impact on bass fishermen or bass as the jig-and-pork combination. This outfit has been a major and important part of my bass fishing for years. And even though I have used them for years, even before I fished plastic worms, it seems that each year I learn something new about fishing the jig - and-pig.

Jigs are presentation lures. That is, the key in using them successfully is presenting them properly to the fish. Essentially, that presentation comes as the jig-and-pig falls, which means it is a fairly easy lure to learn to use.

Basically, you need only about three different weights of jigs for different water temperature, water clarity and the type of cover you will be fishing. Once you cover these conditions, you will have all the jigs you need.

Popular sizes for all depths include: 1/8- and 1/4-ounce for shallow water (depths of 10 feet or less); 3/8-ounce (for depths of 10 to 20 feet); and 1/2- to 3/4-ounce for depths over 20 feet. Another important part of the jig is the pork, and you should have a good assortment of colors and at least three sizes and shapes.

The most productive sizes for nearly all conditions include both the junior and senior sizes of the Strike King Bo-Hawg Frog, Pigtail and Bo-Leech. Naturally, it's smart to experiment with the different sizes and lengths to find out which will produce best.

I've seen one size produce great results and an hour later you couldn't buy a strike on it. But by making a change in the size of the pork, it would change the overall look and action of the jig — and it would start catching fish again.

It is smart to experiment with different jig weights and pork combinations and a super place is a swimming pool or clear-water pond. This kind of experiment can teach you a lot. You aren't fishing, so you are free to concentrate on learning the technique. You will be surprised at how the sink, feel and action of a particular combination change with different sizes of weights and pork. Even better, have someone cast while you watch from. You will see and understand more and thereby improve your jig fishing.

Regardless of the size jig you use, it is important to remember that a jig-and-pork combination is an eye-contact lure. By that I

mean, it is used in a stained, or even better, in a clear-water situation. It has practically no vibration, but many jigs have a built-in rattle and can produce well in shallow muddy water.

I hear a lot of fishermen complaining about missing too many bass on a jig. Here's a tip that will improve those misses. It involves the angle of the hook.

Jigs are made with the hook point pointing in slightly or back towards the hook shaft — which means, you are going to miss

Bootlegger jig and pork frog

some fish. To eliminate this use your pliers to bend the point out slightly (to provide a better bite). Now, put the jig in your hand and simply close your fist around it. The point of the hook should start to stick into your palm. If you feel the point, it is ready for the water.

I can't begin to tell you just how effective this combination is. I'm sure the jig alone would produce a few fish, but by adding pork, it enhances the overall look of it 100 percent. Pork just adds something to a bait. What it does is extends the lure, giving it a streamline look that is very appealing. It adds buoyancy, which allows for greater lift and a slower fall — allowing you to work the lure extremely slow, giving it greater action and more lifelike appearance. Plus, its greatest factor is its texture and taste.

The texture feels alive and a bass will try to eat it. This pork contains sodium chloride. Chlorides are a basic component of blood, so a good salty taste definitely tastes like something live. This is probably the most significant flavor cue that tells the fish it is food. This is why they'll hold on to it longer.

Many times, you won't feel a strike when a bass hits a jig. You will feel only a sluggish weight on the other end. Just a slight pull on your rod tip will start the hook penetrating, especially if it is sharp (like the laser-sharp hooks on Strike King's Bootlegger jigs.

Max Baer admires a timber bass caught on a jig-and-pig

As I said earlier, a jig to me is a presentation lure and its main presentation is its fall. You will find that the majority of strikes occur as this bait drops or falls back to the bottom. And my most productive way in fishing it is to make soft accurate casts and let the jig fall straight to the bottom, — or to the top of submerged cover. Once it settles, I lift my rod tip once, bringing the jig up several inches and letting it fall again. If this doesn't earn a strike, I lift it again and as it falls the second time, I'll usually twitch it very lightly by moving my wrist and letting the jig fall again.

I will normally repeat this motion again several times and then reel it in and cast again. However, if cover is present and my lure is climbing through it, I will usually yo-yo it up and down very slowly, bumping it through the branches one limb at a time. When fishing the lure this way, the strike may be so light that all you feel is a heavy sensation on your line. When this happens you had better be ready to set the hook. Jig fishing demands a lot of concentration. You need to be thinking "strike" the second the lure hits the water and begins to sink.

For years, many anglers have thought that the jig-and-pork combinations were wintertime lures. Well, let me tell you, this is not the case. This combination is a highly productive lure 12 months of the year. However, I will admit I do much better with it when the water temperature is below 70 degrees.

Regardless of when you decide to use it, you must fish it with a ton of confidence. Speaking of confidence, let's spend a second or two discussing that all-important subject —color. Color has become so important in the success of catching or not catching fish. Certain colors definitely have their place and I don't believe there is a color made that won't catch a fish. But at times, certain colors are more visible than others.

This depends on the amount of available light. Light controls the shape, size and color of anything beneath the surface.

I can't stress enough the importance of using a jig with the sharpest hook point possible. As sharp as the Eagle Claw Lazer Point hook is, it is smart to sharpen it periodically. It takes only a few seconds to fashion the ideal point.

In truth, the best and strongest point is round and it always has been. It is sharper because it's a true point. It is stronger and easier to penetrate because its round-cross section allows it to be fashioned with included angles of only 12 degrees.

One of the least-known, yet most vital facts in fishing is that fishermen don't set hooks, fish do. Now, this doesn't mean that you can afford to dispense with the firm hookset that has become so much a part of bass fishing. Studies have shown that the most experienced anglers generate only about 5 to 7 pounds of force at the end of the line with their best hooksetting efforts (when using monofilament line at 30 to 50 feet). The angler-generated hooking force most often only starts the set — while the fish during the first few seconds before the hook can be dislodged finishes the job. Sharp hook points penetrate more easily and are harder to dislodge.

Although many jigs are fished only during the winter, as stated previously, I've had a great deal of success using them the other eight months of the year in all parts of the country. If you try jigs enough, I know you will, too. Without question, the jig-and-pork combinations are consistent bass-catchers if rigged and presented properly. Only by improving our awareness of this fact can we achieve our goals of becoming the best bass anglers we can be.

CHAPTER 15

THE ART OF DEEP CRANKING

As my good friend and veteran outdoor writer, Tim Tucker, once wrote, "Over the past decade, the deep-diving crankbait has won over a legion of followers that stretch from one end of this country to the other. Crankbait fishing has become a real art to dedicated diving lure fishermen, who have taken the time and effort to learn its intricacies. These knowledgeable anglers have taken the crankbait from its 'dummy-bait' reputation to an advanced form of angling.

"In the hands of a talented fisherman who understands the principles of advanced deep-water crankbaiting, these diving baits are the most versatile of all fishing tools. With the proper education and enough practice, it is possible to catch bass in places you could never reach, places you had avoided or places where you never fished before."

I couldn't agree more when it comes to the art of fishing these high-percentage lures. In this chapter, we will be discussing the hows, whens and wheres of deep cranking, ideal line weights, best type of lure, proper rod and length, best type of reel and more.

With super-deep cranking, you need to understand the laws of physics. There are four requirements for extra deep cranking: a long cast, light line, long rod and proper lure.

A long rod that's 7 to 7 1/2 feet in length, accomplishes eight tasks. It allows:

√ For more casting distance.
√ Allows you to cover more water.
√ Allows your bait to achieve greater depth.
√ Keeps the lure in the strike zone longer.
√ Allows you to move more line quicker.
√ Allows for a better hookset from a distance.
√ Provides an even shock-absorber action (like a fly rod).
√ Allows more leverage on the fish during the fight.

Mark Davis got the maximum depth out of Bomber's new Fat Free Shad to win the 1995 BASS Masters Classic.

Another important consideration is the size of line. The size of line used dictates depth — not in regards to the pound-test of it, but the actual diameter of the line. The larger the diameter of the line, the more depth-robbing friction that is created as the line is being pulled through the water.

With deep cranking, keep in mind that whatever line test you use, it is important to consider the actual diameter of the line. My choice for deep cranking is Stren MagnaThin, which has the smallest diameter for each pound-test rating. Example: 12 pound test MagnaThin has an outside diameter of about 8-pound test regular monofilament.

The final part of those four requirements is choosing the proper lure. The best I've ever fished is Bomber's new deep-diver called the Fat Free Shad.

This lure is considerably different from most deep-diving crankbaits. First of all, it is made of polycarbonate, which is practically indestructible. It comes with a very unique lip that allows it to dive vertically quickly (rather than horizontally) when you start your retrieve. The outside edges of the lip have a kick-out point that allows the bait to dart off objects without hanging. And the sound chamber built into the lure creates a highly effective inviting sound.

Another interesting thing about it, is that it has tremendous buoyancy, which allows it to back up quickly on a stop-and-go retrieve. Perhaps its greatest attribute which makes it so effective, is its flat-sided body. Because of the hydrodynamics involved, a flat-sided plug provides a fast tight-wiggle action that you just can't find in a round bait — plus it will dive with less effort and resistance (meaning it won't work you to death). This bait is large and I believe that this is sometimes a distinct advantage. That is simply because there is more room for contact and less margin for error. Also, it's easier for the fish to see.

When the bait wiggles back and forth, a flat-sided plug has to displace more water than a rounded plug to achieve the same side-to-side swing.

Plus, there's more water resistance against a flat surface than a rounded one, and this keeps the bait from wobbling very much to either side. A rounded plug is like a round-bottom boat. A round boat will rock from side-to-side, almost uncontrollably in rough water, because it has no resistance to the water and the same is true of a rounded bait.

Now, I don't want you to think that fat baits are out and thin is in, because they're not. There are times when a tight fast wiggle is more appealing to the bass than a wider, slower wobble and other times it's not. This is something you'll have to experiment with.

I will tell you this, though. I think the terrific action of these plugs combined with the extensive vibration they produce makes them much easier for the bass to locate. When the fish can't see a crankbait very well, they can still find this plug. Something else I've found out is that I seem to have better success in colder water with fat-bodied baits and flat-sided baits in warmer water. When fishing flat-sided lures like the Fat Free Shad, you will find that they don't fight you. You can cast them all day without tiring and the weight of this plug allows you to cast it accurately on windy days without worrying about it sailing on you.

A discussion about deep cranking would not be complete without mentioning the best type of reel for this application. Over the past 15 years or so, reel manufacturers have made tremendous strides in increasing the take-up speed of their products. Today, 5 to 1 and even 6 to 1 high-speed reels are as common as knee-high tackle boxes. With all of this, don't get the idea that faster means better when it comes to crankbait fishing. More speed does not necessarily translate into more depth. You need to realize that the high-speed reels are moving your lure almost twice as fast as a slower-ratio reel will.

Don't make the mistake of believing that the faster you crank, the deeper the lure goes. Two critical things happen when you try to burn the lure with a fast retrieve.

Cranking expert Rick Clunn scores on a flat-sided, deep-diving crankbait.

First, it affects the action of the lure and, secondly, it won't run at the same depth. Once you overcome the buoyancy factor of the lure itself, it will run at its deepest from that point. To gain maximum depth control is usually a moderate, comfortable retrieve.

Let me tell you why a lower gear ratio reel works best for this kind of fishing:

√ It provides a slower retrieve speed and more power.

√ It forces the angler to fish a crankbait at a slower speed.

√ It maximizes depth and lure performance.

√ The lower gear ratio takes less effort to retrieve with high-resistance lures (causing less fatigue on the fisherman).

√ A 5.4 to 1 gear ratio reel works well for deep-diving crankbaits and is ideal for providing the best lure action and speed. A 6 to 1 ratio reel retrieves about 28 inches of line per turn of the reel handle. A 5 to 1 gear ratio takes up 22 inches. And a 4.4 to 1 reel brings in 18 inches per handle turn.

Slower retrieves allow the lure to achieve greater depth by allowing the bait to work vertically — not horizontally — allowing a more deliberate, natural bait action as it digs the bottom and bumps structure. And finally, it keeps the bait in the strike-zone longer.

Armed with the proper tackle and lure, deep cranking does not have to be the chore that it once was.

CHAPTER 16

THE ALLURE OF BUZZBAITS

Someone once said that buzzbaits are silly lures. Maybe they are, but what does that matter as long as bass like them?

As funny as they may look and act, they are one of the most exciting bass lures of all to use.

When you really think about it, it doesn't look like anything natural, especially in the watery world of the bass. But as we know, bass are not locked into only a selective diet.

When you retrieve this bait across the surface, the turning, churning blade gurgles steadily. It's the only lure in the family of topwaters that is constantly on the move creating a commotion that suggests it is some form of life scurrying for survival. But regardless of how it looks or sounds or whether bass react to it out of anger, hunger, curiosity or reflex, they are prone to bust it.

My favorite buzzbait is a 1/2-ounce Buzz King, which comes equipped with a Mirage silicone skirt, an Eagle Claw Lazer Sharp hook and a triple-diamond designed chrome or colored propeller blade.

And of all the buzzbaits I've ever used, the Buzz King is far and away my favorite simply because of its balance, profile and sound. The blade design allows me to retrieve it as fast as I want or crawl it at a snail's pace across the surface, which I feel is the most effective presentation. By adding a frog-like pork chuck to the hook, it gives the lure more buoyancy for an even slower presentation.

There is just something magical about a buzzbait. It will definitely provoke strikes when other lures fail. I've seen the time — many times in fact — when bass were too inactive to bite some lures, but would eat up a buzzbait.

There are advantages to fishing a bait of this type. You can cover a lot of water quickly with it, attract fish that cannot see your

Just how good are buzzbaits? Good enough to win national tournaments, as Florida pro Larry Lazoen and the Potomac River bass can attest.

offering, fish it over, around and through many forms of cover that other lures would be difficult to fish. Also, buzzbaits have a tremendous reputation for attracting large fish. That's not to say they don't appeal to smaller bass, because they will in a mighty big way. But buzzers seem to have a sound that really turn on big bass.

Everybody loves buzzbait fishing. I believe the reason this lure is so popular is because it is so highly visible. You actually see the strike and that keeps you on your toes. The anticipation of knowing the strike could come at anytime, can and does make you over-react when you see the water wake up as the fish strikes — making you jerk too quickly, snatching the lure away from the fish. It's hard to do, but if you pause until you feel the fish, you will improve your strike-catch ratio tremendously. Try to remember to jerk by feel, rather than by sight.

Bass are going to miss a fair percentage of their strikes, but many will chase and hit repeatedly if the lure isn't jerked away from them.

Speaking of missing bass on buzzbaits, here is something you can do that will reduce those kinds of problems. Missed strikes aren't always a bad thing. There are times when bass won't aggressively bust a buzzbait, but they will make curious swipes at it. These fish often can be caught by having a spare rod ready and immediately casting a slower drop-bait of some sort — like a Pork-O, plastic worm or jig-and-pork combination — right to the spot where the strike occurred.

Used in this fashion, a buzzbait makes a good fish locator, even if the bass have to be caught on something else.

Let me tell you about the best presentation I've found with this lure. Many fishermen have the tendency to work the lure too fast. The more you want to catch a bass, usually the faster you fish the bait. It's just a natural tendency. This rapid race across the surface may work on some occasions, but, more often than not, bass prefer a slow pace.

The slowest that a buzzbait will run and still stay on the surface is ideal. The slow rate can be best obtained by using a three-blade buzzer with a frog-chunk (and keeping your rod tip at about the 10 o'clock position).

What is it about the buzzbait that catches largemouths so well? I believe it's the sound. That is the key factor in attracting fish. Some buzzbaits attract more fish than others and I believe the reason for this is that some produce a positive sound versus a negative one. The Buzz King seems to produce a positive, bass-attracting noise.

It is amazing to me just how far a fish can hear sound. But when you think about it, it's really not that hard to understand. Water is a much better conductor of sound than air. Sound travels only 1,087 feet per second in the air, but zips 4,800 feet per second in water and thousands of times more efficiently. In case you were wondering, 4,800 feet per second is almost a mile. It's no wonder that fish can hear so well.

Beside a buzzbait having good sound, every bass lure that catches fish consistently has other features that help attract the bass' attention. Some of these would be size, color, shape, action and as I said earlier, a slow movement on the surface.

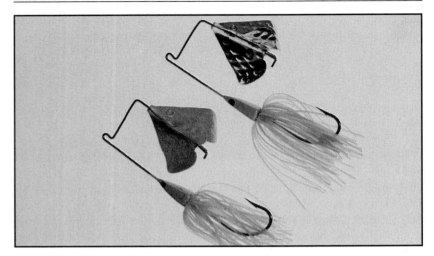

Some buzzbaits, like the Buzz King, attract more fish because they produce a positive, bass-attracting noise. It's amazing how far away bass seem to be able to hear certain buzzers.

Catching a bass on the surface is a real special way of fishing. When you can trick a surface feeder into striking, you have experienced one of the greatest thrills in angling. That is especially true with a lure that looks and acts so silly.

Buzzbaits are simply tops in my book.

CHAPTER 17

SPINNERBAITS DOWN DEEP

When we think of spinnerbait fishing, most bass fishermen automatically associate it with shallow water. It is a mighty effective lure for fishing depths of 1 to 5 feet. But I can tell you from experience that spinnerbaits are also consistent fish-producers for catching deep-water bass.

Of course, "deep" is a relative term. On a highland reservoir, deep water is in excess of 30 feet and shallow water is 15 feet and less. But in a lowland lake, anything over 15 feet would be considered extremely deep.

To me, deep means the level at which most lures become ineffective. And a spinnerbait is a viable tool with a good presentation that catches fish at almost all depths.

When bass are inactive, using a large spinnerbait can be a highly productive tactic. You get reaction strikes rather than feeding strikes during those non-aggressive times. And the flash and vibration of the blade and the action of the skirt triggers strikes in a big way.

When fishing deep, your choice of lures is limited. Anything below the 20-foot mark can be fished effectively with only five different lures: plastic worm, jig-and-pork combination, grub, jigging spoon and spinnerbait.

Although a jigging spoon can be a good lure for deep-structure fishing, deep-water bass can be stubborn and in a negative mood. In that case, there are lures that can be more effective. The spinnerbait is one of them. At times, it has an advantage over the spoon because it has a slower, more appealing, even tantalizing action. And it gives you the same type of fall that you get with a jig-and-pork. Also, the blade gives it more vibration and visibility. It

Tate Bowden knows deep-spinnerbaiting requires less effort than other forms of structure fishing. And it obviously works.

moves slowly enough to give the bass time to look it over and size it up — so they are more likely to attack it as it crawls along.

I should emphasize that I am not implying that a jig, grub, spoon and worm are not excellent lures for probing the deeper depths. They certainly are. What I am trying to stress is that you need to be versatile and try them all, because there are going to be times when one will out-perform the other. But at times, you will be hard-pressed to find a lure that will out-perform a spinnerbait.

For fishing a spinnerbait in deep water, my choice is a single-spin Strike King Spin-Dance. It features a silicone mirage skirt, 4/0 Eagle Claw Lazer Sharp hook, an American-made Spin-

Eze ball-bearing and a 4.5 turtle-shell prism blade. It is a perfectly balanced bait that is ideal for fishing deep structure.

I will use the 3/8-ounce size at any depth — as long as I can feel it (simply because I can work it slower). Should the wind pick up and the bass move even deeper, I will switch to a heavier spinnerbait, like a 1/2-ounce bait.

The vibration on this particular spinnerbait is tremendous and can be felt distinctly through the rod tip. Whenever the blade stops pulsating, chances are a bass has taken the spinnerbait and you need to set the hook quickly.

When fishing a spinnerbait down deep, it is important to pay close attention to what your lure is doing at all times. A good, sensitive rod will help you feel the bottom as well as the vibration of the lure. It is a really easy lure to fish, but takes persistence and confidence to be successful with this technique. Patience is the key word here. It takes time for the lure to drop 20 feet. And it takes patience to slow-roll the spinnerbait along the bottom. But if you are willing to work at it, I know you will be consistently rewarded.

A proven tactic when fishing a heavy spinnerbait begins with the proper position. If the terrain allows it, position the boat in shallow water and then cast out into deep water (so that your retrieve is up-hill). This will enable you to work the lure with less effort and cover the bottom depth much easier. This is especially productive when the bass are holding tight to the cover or bottom. Another advantage to positioning your boat shallow and casting out (versus positioning out deep and casting to the shallower area) occurs once you have hooked a bass. There is a tendency for other bass to follow the hooked fish. By pulling the fish from deep to shallow, the trailing bass move a certain distance, but then return quickly to their original location. But when you hook a fish and bring him out over the deeper water, the following fish become disoriented and it takes them much longer to regroup back to their original spot.

I've seen this happen many, many times. And I know for a fact that you will catch more fish from a deep-water area by fishing from shallow to deep.

Have you ever wondered why fishing rods come in all different lengths? Believe it or not, all have their place. A 7 1/2-foot rod will out-perform a 5 1/2-foot rod in some cases. A 5 1/2-footer will out-perform a 7 1/2-footer in other situations.

Let's discuss the advantages of using a longer rod (6 1/2 to 7 1/2 feet in length.)

For years, the trend was for those lengthy, long-handled poles to be standard tackle for flipping, which gave fishermen the ability to present lures at close range to bass and in thick tight cover.

More and more anglers are using them for more than just flipping. Longer rods are becoming more accepted all the time as substitutes for basic 5-, 5 1/2- and 6-foot casting rods. Although a fishing rod is a lever, its advantage is one of speed, rather than one of power.

What this means is that fishing rods, depending on their length, expedite the energy of the hooksetting motions. The longer rod pulls the line farther with the same effort than a shorter rod. And this will move the hook farther and quicker. Simply put, you will improve your strike-catch ratio more with a longer rod than with a standard 5 1/2-footer. The rod needs to be fairly stiff, too. The more the rod bends under pressure, the less energy is available to move the hook.

The longer rod helps you get a big fish up and out of thick places — simply because you can move a fish farther and have more control once you hook him. Another plus to the added length is that it offers lots of opportunities for presenting the bait that the shorter rod doesn't. And the longer length causes the tip to travel farther on the cast, resulting in longer casts. This

A 3/8- to 1/2-ounce Strike King Spin-Dance with a 4.5 turtle-shell prism blade is ideal for slow-rolling deep cover.

advantage is most obvious when you are trying to reach a breaking fish or perhaps a school of bass chasing bait on the surface. Another advantage is depth. Using a crankbait, you will be able to fire it out a long distance, which will allow for greater depth control. Also, the rod allows you to reel down and punch off a lure that is hung up on cover, many times.

For deep-spinnerbaiting, a fine diameter, 14-pound test Stren Easy Cast monofilament line is a good all-around choice. It is thin enough to let the lure get deep, yet strong enough to handle a good fish in cover.

As I said earlier, fishing deep with a heavy spinnerbait demands less physical effort than many other forms of bass fishing. It does require concentration and an abundance of patience. If you just can't wait for the bait to sink deep or are unable to maintain slow, methodical retrieves, you will have little success. But if you have what it takes to slow down and probe the depths, you just might catch more bass in deep water on spinnerbaits than you ever did with these lures in the shallows — especially during those inactive times.

CHAPTER 18

UNDERSTANDING CRANKBAIT DYNAMICS

Do you want to discover a fishing lure that is really easy to use in locating bass? One that can be used almost 12 months of the year, can be fished shallow or deep, and doesn't require any special techniques for setting the hook? Got any idea what it is?

Well, if you said a crankbait you would be 100 percent correct. It is a lure you can cover lots of water with quickly.

It stands to reason, the more productive water you can fish in a day, the more the odds will be in your favor — and the more bass will have the chance of seeing your lure. And the chances are much greater that you will catch more bass.

Naturally this depends greatly on the location you choose, the depth you fish and the lure, color and presentation you use.

In this chapter, we will be discussing several tips to help you understand more about these terrific lures and how you can benefit by using them. We will be discussing the importance of line size, speed and depth control, distance of casts, lip position and design, and how water temperature affects the crankbait.

One of my longtime favorite crankbaits is the Bomber Fat A. It's a dandy. I like it so much that I helped design two colors that I find really productive for most fishing situations — the Shad Ghost and Bengal Tiger.

There is no doubt about it, crankbaits are among the easiest lures to learn to fish since the action of the lure often attracts a strike (regardless of the retrieve). This makes it an excellent choice — even for a beginner.

Here's something you might find interesting. Many fishermen believe that the faster you crank a bait of this type, the deeper it will dive. This is totally wrong. For a crankbait to gain its maximum depth, a slow retrieve will send it deep. Once it hits the surface, five to six fast turns of the reel handle will get it started and a slow to moderate retrieve will allow it to dive to its maximum depth.

Water pressure must flow off both sides of the lip equally in order for the lure to dive properly. When you use a fast retrieve, the water pressure begins to flow off the front portion of the lip, creating a wet-stick effect that restricts the depth, as well as the action.

Naturally there are other things to consider such as the line size you use, the distance of your cast, the position and design of the lip and even water temperature.

Line size plays a very important role in the depth you obtain with a crankbait. You are simply going to get more depth with lighter line. The reason is that the lighter the line, the smaller the diameter, so there is less friction coming through the water. The heavier the line, the more resistance because there's more friction. You would be surprised at the difference that 10-pound test line and 20-pound test make. With the average crankbait, you can get a couple of extra feet of depth with 10-pound test and in many situations, an extra two feet can be crucial. But there is a point when you use below 10-pound test that you can actually lose a little depth because of line stretch.

Another problem created by using heavier line with crank-baits is the possibility of altering that all important vibration pattern. Anything that moves through the water vibrates to some degree, and line also makes noise coming through the water. The diameter of heavier line can change the vibration pattern of a crankbait. Naturally, the smaller the lure, the more critical the problem becomes — both in terms of depth and vibration. Larger lures do not present that much of a problem.

You also sacrifice depth if your crankbait is not running dead-center.

Let's talk about distance of cast for a minute. It is basic geometry that the farther you cast a crankbait, the deeper it will dive. Using a long rod (6 to 7 feet in length) helps gain better depth control. The longer length causes the tip to travel farther on the cast resulting in greater distance.

Now there are also drawbacks to long casting. For one thing, you don't have near as much hooksetting power. Also, you can't feel the lure as well as you can at close range. One thing that affects this is line stretch. The longer monofilament line stays in the water, the more moisture it absorbs. All monofilament stretches and thoroughly wet lines stretch more than dry lines — as much as 30 percent.

Even if stretch equates to only a few inches at the end of a 50-foot cast, it can sap the power of the hookset. To help limit stretch, it is best to alternate rods every half hour or so. Naturally, this stretch also affects your feel and depth control.

Another thing that'll affect depth control is lip position and design. The type of lip determines how deep a crankbait will dive.

I helped design two new colors of Bomber's Fat A crankbait.

Many fishermen believe that a crankbait with a sloping lip dives the deepest. But actually, one with a lip extending straight off the nose or front runs deeper. The size of the lip in comparison to the body also affects the running depth. The longer and wider the lip, the deeper it will dive.

Water temperature can affect depth, too. You heard me right — even water temperature has an effect on crankbait depth. The warmer water gets, the thinner it becomes; the colder water gets, the thicker or more dense it becomes. Obviously then, a crankbait will dive a little deeper in thinner (or warmer) water.

Two of the most important controls a fisherman has at his disposal are depth and speed. Depth is critically important. If the lure is not worked on the fish's depth level, it may not hit it unless the bass is extremely active. Getting the lure down to the bass' depth level is just as important as making an accurate cast to him. Recognize that once the lure is down, your retrieve — whether fast or slow — should always be erratic. You have to vary your retrieve to determine the fish's mood at that time. Once the lure is down, try slow-to-fast, or fast-to-pause-to-fast, or even fast-to-slow-to-stop-to-fast. The key word is control. Speed control is important and must be learned, but it pays off handsomely. I guarantee it.

In cold water (or when bass are super-inactive), retrieve speed needs to be much slower, because during such times, bass are more sluggish. Now in warmer waters, your retrieve speeds can be faster; however, just because the weather is warmer doesn't necessarily mean that fast retrieves are the answer. Remember, you have to vary your retrieve.

The little guy called the Bomber Fat A has the four most important characteristics in a crankbait: wobble, buoyancy, sound and shape.

You sacrifice depth when your crankbait isn't running true.
Quality baits like the Fat Free Shad can be easily adjusted.

When fishing a crankbait, correct presentation and depth are vital to success. With the Fat A, I can use 10-pound test line and reach depths close to 12 feet on a long cast. Heavier lines won't allow the lure to go as deep due to line drag. With 14-pound test, 10- and 12-foot depths are possible. Moving up to 17- to 20-pound test line, I can hit depths of 8 feet with this bait without much effort.

There are certain things that I look for in a good crankbait. First, is looks. It has got to look good in order for me to buy it and use it. That sounds silly, but I feel that's important. It's part of the confidence game. Secondly, I want a crankbait that has the proper weight to accurately cast it a long distance — even into a strong wind. Third, I want a bait that will vertically dive quickly and does not create a lot of resistance on the retrieve. Fourth, I want it to create a good wiggle once it gets down. Fifth, it must have strong, sharp hooks. Sixth, I want it to produce an inviting sound. Seventh, and most of all, bass must be attracted to it in a big way. That's why I like the Fat A. It's a wonderful lure that really produces lots of bass for me.

Another major feature I like is the shape of these baits They are fat in shape and resemble the predominant forage which is shad in most of the lakes I fish — both thread fin and gizzard. The shape of the Fat A looks very similar to the shad. In bodies of water where minnows, chubs and smelt are the main forage, I do better with a long narrow bait. And where shiners or herring are found, I have better success with a similar shaped bait.

I've never been one that believes in the theory of matching the hatch. Why would I cast a 1 1/2-inch shad-colored crankbait into a school of bass that are chasing a pod of several thousand 1 1/2-inch shad? The competition is simply too great. I want to throw something that looks similar in shape but not size. It needs to be noticeably different, where it can be seen.

Perhaps the most important point of any crankbait is its hooking ability once the lure has been struck.

The strong and sharp hooks that Bomber uses on this bait are called Excaliber counter-rotating trebles. This is a hook that delivers a significant hooking advantage over standard treble hooks. They were designed with a counter-rotating angle in each hook. Each of the two free points travel counter-clockwise once contact is made with one point. The movement of the hook points result in at least one other point coming into contact with the striking fish.

This will increase your hook-to-landing ratio by at least 30 percent. It is perhaps the most effective treble hook ever developed.

Another advantage to the Fat A is its wide lip, which helps in making it more weedless. On the retrieve, the lure runs in a head-down position so that the lip makes contact with an obstruction before the hooks do. As a result, the lure usually deflects off solid objects before the hooks can become snagged.

The Fat A comes in five different sizes and weights, from 1 1/4 to 2 1/2 inches in length and weights from 1/16- to 1/2-ounce. All have their place depending on the depth you're fishing.

In selecting a crankbait, it is wise to select one like the Fat A, especially when bass are inactive and want a slow, stop-and-go retrieve. The fat shape makes it more buoyant and that makes it highly effective, simply because it backs up quickly when you stop your retrieve, and that is extremely important when bass are picky.

Despite living in Florida, Roland Martin has learned to appreciate the allure of the lead jigging spoon — and it's not just for the coldest times of the year.

CHAPTER 19

JIGGING UP SPOON-FED BASS

Another of my favorite baits is a jigging spoon. It appears to be an ordinary shiny piece of metal with a treble hook attached. But when it is placed underwater and fished the proper way, it appears to come alive and closely imitates one of the bass' favorite foods — shad.

I'd like to share some helpful tips on how to spoon-feed bass in deep water. Two of the most important tools for this technique are a good map and a sensitive depthfinder. The map will show you the general area where good underwater structure is located and the graph will help you pinpoint it further (as well as show the depth, available cover and even any resident largemouths).

Without those two tools, an angler has only his knowledge of a specific lake and possibly a good bit of luck to rely on when it comes to locating fish. Having the right tools will permit you to cover a greater area of water, as well as eliminate dead, fishless water. To me, the use of modern electronics is one of the most important aspects of all bass fishing.

For years, the jigging spoon has been considered by many as primarily a late-fall and winter lure. But I'm totally convinced that it will produce year-round if it is fished where the bass can see it. The clearer the water, the better it produces.

Many fishermen don't know how to use a spoon properly. The amount of movement you give the spoon can determine whether or not it produces anything. You have to play with the action. In other words, experiment enough to find the pulse that produces strikes. One of the most productive presentations is one that I call a "double-hop" retrieve. All I do is lift the spoon on a 12- to 24-inch pattern and, at the top of the lift, I twitch my rod twice — then let the lure flutter back while holding a slight tension. There will be times, however, when if you move it more than 6 inches, the fish won't touch it. And I've seen lots of days (especially days when the bass were inactive) when the right action amounted simply to "no action" at all. In those cases, lift the spoon a couple of inches and then hold it completely still. You will be sitting there and all of a sudden the strike will occur.

I'm convinced that lead spoons like this 3/4-ounce Diamond Design model by Strike King will produce year-round if it is fished where bass can see it.

The key to spoon fishing is being able to tell exactly what is going on down there. The mistake many fishermen make is to give too much movement and action to the bait. When bass are active, movement is not all that critical.

The spoon I like to use is Strike King's 3/4-ounce Diamond Design model that produces lots of reflection. It also has a Spin-Eze ball-bearing on the line tie to prevent line twist. It's an ideal weight and has a perfect fluttering action.

Most strikes typically occur as the bait is falling, so it is vital that you stay in touch with it at all times. Most of the time, you want the lure to fall freely so that it maintains its natural fluttering action. Don't restrict its descent by tight-lining it. On the other hand, if you let it fall on total slack line, you will get hits that you won't detect.

The key is to develop a rhythm with the bait. Once you have established a rhythm for that particular time and situation, remember to lower the rod tip at the same rate that the spoon is falling (so that your line remains relatively tight yet does not hamper the fall of the spoon). Typically, most strikes on a spoon are somewhat faint. The sensation is very much like you tickling your fingers together or someone tapping your line with their rod tip. Bass are not going to hold on to a jigging spoon long, so whack them as soon as you feel the strike.

Vertical fishing with a jigging spoon is really a fun way to fish. They are easy to work, exciting to use, and precision lures that are unmatched in their effectiveness on bass holding along deep-water structure. Another thing about this lure is that it is one of a few

Doubling the Survey Area of a Depthfinder

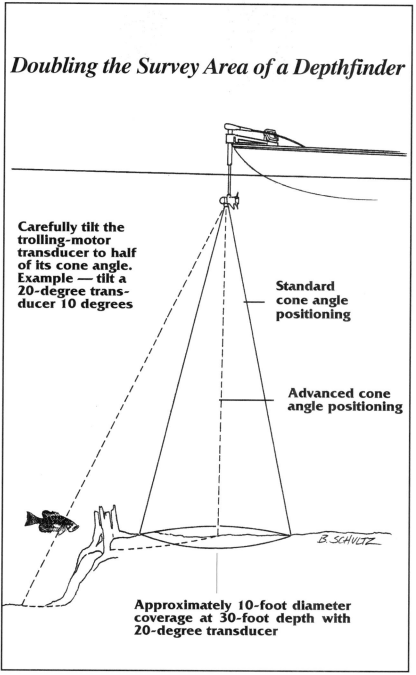

Carefully tilt the trolling-motor transducer to half of its cone angle. Example — tilt a 20-degree transducer 10 degrees

Standard cone angle positioning

Advanced cone angle positioning

Approximately 10-foot diameter coverage at 30-foot depth with 20-degree transducer

B. SCHULTZ

Bernie Schultz

lures I know of that a fisherman can position precisely in the strike zone — and then keep it there for as long as he wants.

When bass are shallow, dozens of lures will cover that territory more efficiently. But when bass drop below 15 feet or so, the jigging spoon is a bad dude.

Let me share with you a little tip I use (especially when I'm vertical fishing deep water) that allows me to double the survey area I'm fishing. It is all done with the aid of my depthfinder (see diagram on preceding page). The Eagle liquid-crystal unit I use is equipped with a 20-degree transducer that is mounted on the lower unit of my trolling motor. The 20-degree angle cone covers an area approximately one-third of the depth. In other words, at a depth of 30 feet, the unit will show a 10-foot diameter which is actually a 5-foot-bottom radius at that depth. By tilting the transducer 10 degrees, the search area will be doubled and out in front of the boat in whatever direction the trolling motor is pointed. What this does is give you the advantage of seeing structure and fish before you are directly over or past them and allows you to adjust much quicker and pinpoint targets exactly.

A word of caution: Only tilt the transducer to half of its cone angle. Tilt it only 10 degrees on a 20-degree transducer. Otherwise, your depth will be off and you won't have a true feeling of what you're seeing.

As I said earlier, jigging spoons are fun to fish, easy to work and exciting to use. If you are ever to become proficient at deep-water bass fishing, this is one lure you must master.

CHAPTER 20

ULTRALIGHT BASS BASICS

To paraphrase an advertising cliche´, half the fun is in the catching. This fact underlies the growing interest in ultralight fishing now sweeping the country.

Ultralights are the small spinning or spin-cast reels that nestle in the palm of the hand, hold sensitive line in the 2- to 4-pound test range and cast tiny lures — most of which are under the 1/4-ounce mark. The rods are limber, lightweight sticks that usually measure 5 to 5 1/2 feet in length. Using mini-gear magnifies the challenge and maximizes the fun in bass fishing.

You can see it in trout streams´, where anglers have discovered that a 1-pound rainbow trout at the end of a 2-pound test line takes on all the dimensions of a fighting fury six times its weight. In oxbows, sloughs, lakes and ponds across the country, the focus is on the scrappy bluegill, a formidable fighter in its weight class that becomes a runaway dump truck when hooked with ultralight gear. An 8- to 10-ounce bluegill can provide a severe test for the most experienced angler, giving the fish a fighting chance by using the ultralight approach.

The wisp of a "willow switch" rod arched sharply that looks like the letter C and the tiny spinning reel whirls with a screech. The sewing-thread size of monofilament line, hardly visible to the angler's eyes, will cut V- and Z- shaped wakes as the fish cuts toward deeper water. With every lunge, the small reel whines sharply and the fisherman tightens his grip on the straining rod handle.

Using only light tackle, the angler acknowledges the fish's right to a fighting chance, and the fish gives its best effort —forcing the angler to do the same. This is the mystique of ultralight fishing. It appeals to the best sporting instinct of the bass enthusiast.

Fishermen rediscover the exhilaration of their long-ago youth when they master a 2-pound bass within the limitations set by ultralight tackle. There's a subtle sophistication inherent in ultralight fishing.

Experienced anglers sense that immediately during the first few casts with the fine ultralight gear now on the market. Combining

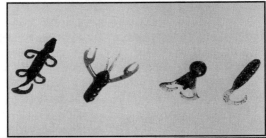

Ultralight fishing for bass is sporting and productive, thanks to deadly little lures like Riverside's Micro Air Series critters.

light line with the delicate sensory capabilities of graphite rods, and the fisherman suddenly has enhanced his ability to interpret the faint vibrations that emanate from the unseen prey.

This is the age of ultralight. A decade ago, the major tackle manufacturers provided the only ultralight spinning rigs. This changed dramatically as new priorities and technology soared in a wave of ultralight spin-cast rigs with the quality and features of larger reels. Many come packaged in light, plastic carrying cases that can be snapped on your belt or placed in a large size pocket.

Manufacturers like Zebco/Quantum have made impressive strides toward creating the ultimate in well-balanced ultralight rods and reels. When purely fun fishing, I enjoy using Quantum's Micro Systems, which might be the most advanced of all ultralight gear. My spinning outfit usually consists of a 4-foot, 6-inch, super-ultralight action rod (MS54SULG) and matching reel (MS1XL). For making long casts, I switch to a 6-foot (MS72SULG) rod.

My wife, Dianne, enjoys catching bass on an ultralight outfit. And, as you can see, she's pretty good at it.

I complete the balanced outfit by selecting the right type of line. A small-diameter line like Stren's MagnaThin is perfect for casting small lures on ultralight tackle.

Today's ultralight angler has a wide choice of lure sizes appropriate to the needs of baby reels and light lines. Many are simply miniaturized versions of long lures familiar to most fishermen, which measure well under 2 inches and weigh from less than 1/4-ounce down to 1/64-ounce.

A real productive small lure for this type of fishing is Bomber's smallest Fat A (3A), which is an ultralight delight. It delivers long, accurate casts and attains a rattling depth of up to 5 feet. It's small enough to be eaten by panfish, but strong enough to bring in a surprisingly big bass.

I've had a ball experimenting with Riverside's Micro Air Series, which is new for 1996. The series includes a tiny grub, crawfish, lizard and an interesting plastic shape called the Micro Air Critter. These are creatures that every ultralight bass enthusiast will love.

Each lure has a patented air chamber that makes them buoyant enough to float a No. 12 hook. That enables the fisherman to work these baits along every single fish-holding spot that he encounters. Each of these little lures have a realistic look and action — with vibrating tails, pinchers and legs that flutter with even a subtle rod movement or the slightest current.

All of this eye-catching tackle and lures, however, is useless until the angler develops the skill that ultralight fishing demands.

The angler, not the equipment, is paramount when tangling with a bass raising cane at the end of a delicate line on a small lure with tiny hooks. You don't simply reel in a fish on ultralight tackle. You learn the true definition of the phrase "playing the fish." You don't horse a fish; the victory is gained by capitalizing on the reel's smooth drag and the rod's whippy flexibility to wear the prey down.

Once you have honed your ultralight skills on an assortment of bluegill, crappie or small bass, there are few challenges beyond your capabilities. Quite a few ultralight anglers stick to their delicate gear when searching out the big boys. They have arrived at a point where they think they can triumph over the big lunkers, or have a fun time trying.

Ultralights are for those anglers who like the difficult things in life. If you want a real challenge and love a good fight regardless of who might come out the winner, then ultralight tackle is the ticket to the ultimate in angling satisfaction.

CHAPTER 21

THE MAKING OF A CLASSIC CRANKBAIT

I'm sure most of you remember as a youngster wanting that very special something. And when you got it, your excitement level was higher than the clouds. Well, let me tell you, it's been a long time since I was a youngster, but my level of excitement is still the same — especially when it comes to a special new lure I've wanted for so long.

Today, I received that very special something, a deep-diving crankbait that has all the qualities to make it the perfect lure for deep water structure. It's a 3/4-ounce, 3-inch lure called the Bomber Fat Free Shad.

You might have heard of this impressive new crankbait. After all, Mark Davis won the 1995 BASS Masters Classic on the Fat Free Shad. You might say that this crankbait made B.A.S.S. history because Davis became the first man ever to win the Angler of the Year and Classic titles in one year.

The Fat Free Shad has a built-in rattler, super buoyancy, a tight wiggle, sharp Excaliber hooks, a straight lip for better depth control, kick-out features on each side of the lip (which we will discuss later), an ideal flat-sided body shape and the most attractive fish catching colors on the market today. It is made of polycarbonate, which is practically indestructible.

Am I excited about this new lure? Yes, I am! You know, there are a few deep-running crankbaits out there that actually do run in the 15-foot range and even fewer that go a little deeper. But the one thing those big-lipped plugs all have in common is that they pull back hard. This means that fishing these lures turns into more of an exercise in survival than a fishing trip.

It was with this in mind that Bomber lure designer Jim Gowing and I began working together to create a deep-running crankbait that would work easily in the 15- to 18- foot range with

Mark Davis got excited about the Fat Free Shad when he received a few samples in his hotel room. His enthusiasm for the lure was rewarded handsomely a month later in the Classic.

great action and yet would not physically stress the equipment or the angler. I'm happy to report that after a year of testing and many prototypes we've accomplished that goal with this exciting new bait.

The Fat Free Shad can reach depths of 14 to 18 feet easily because you can cast this lure for great distances — even in the wind — without worrying about it sailing on you. The first time you cast it, you'll know what I mean.

It is important to remember that the actual running depths of big-lipped crankbaits vary with the length of your cast, the line diameter you use, the retrieve speed, as well as water temperature.

The length of your cast will greatly influence the depth control of your lure. Example: if you make a cast at a distance of 40 feet, the lure will dive deeper than it would, with a 20-foot cast. So, to gain better depth control, your cast should be made farther.

The size of line you use dictates depth — not in regards to the pound-test of it, but the actual diameter of the line. Example: the larger the diameter of the line, the more depth-robbing friction that's created as the line is pulled through the water. Whatever line test you select, disregard the line manufacturer's line strength claim and consider the actual diameter of the line. My choice for deep cranking is Stren MagnaThin, which has the smallest diameter for each pound-test rating. Example: 12-pound test MagnaThin has a diameter of about 8-pound test regular monofilament.

Let's discuss the speed of your retrieve. This, too, has a major bearing on how much depth you gain on a long cast. Burning a deep-diving crankbait is a no-no. To gain the maximum depth of a crankbait, use a slow to moderate retrieve. This will allow the bait to gain its deepest diving depth. For a crankbait to gain its greatest depth, water must flow off of each side of the lip. Burning a crankbait will eliminate this, causing the water to flow off the front of the lip and restricting depth control.

As silly as this might sound, water temperature can also affect running depths. Here's why: cold water is much denser than warm water. In other words, the colder water gets, the thicker it becomes; the warmer water gets, the thinner it becomes. This means, you will get better depth control in 80-degree water, than you will in 60-degree water. This 20-degree change in temperature may only cause your bait to run a foot or so different, but that little difference can have a major impact on whether or not you catch bass.

To gain more depth, your cast should be made farther and your line diameter should be smaller. It is important to remember the main function of a lure isn't to catch fish — it's to find fish. That's what fishermen spend the majority of their time doing on every fishing trip anyway. When covering a lot of water quickly and thoroughly in a limited amount of time, no other lure performs better than a crankbait.

Here is something else I really like about this bait. Once I get it down, I'm looking for it to hit something and deflect off to the side. The shape of the Fat Free Shad bill gives it an almost weedless deflection quality as a result of the kick-out points on each

Bomber Fat Free Shad

side of the lip. I really like that. In other words, when it hits something, the lure kicks out to one side or the other — and I honestly know that sudden, erratic movement often triggers a bass to strike.

I would say that the majority of my crankbait strikes occur when I'm using a stop-and-go retrieve or when it ricochets off cover. As I said, this sudden erratic motion triggers strikes. I believe it appears that the bait is crippled and it is the instinct of a predator to remove the weak creatures. Whether it's a fox or a bass, any predator creature knows that erratic action signals weakness in prey.

An important aspect of deep-cranking with the Fat Free Shad and other crankbaits is the length and action of the rod you use. Most avid bass fishermen prefer long fiberglass rods for crankbait fishing and for good reason: glass is a lot more forgiving than fast-tipped graphite, thus fewer big fish are lost. Graphite for sure provides better feel and control of the lure, but with fiberglass you experience the loss of sensitivity and some control. But the hooking benefits far outweigh the losses. When a bass stops a crankbait, something has to give — either the angler or the rod. Many fishermen are so excited and tend to be so keyed up that they jerk at the instant they first feel the initial bump, thump or tap. With a fiberglass rod, a bass is hooked better, because the lure isn't yanked out of its mouth.

Once I get the lure down, I concentrate intently on what it is doing. When the vibration of the lure changes (which often indicates a strike), it is smart not to react immediately, instead keep reeling until the fish hooks itself. Contrary to what most fishermen think, an angler doesn't want to know when a bass has hit the crankbait until it really has a firm hold.

What a fisherman should look for in a crankbait rod is a fiberglass rod between 6 1/2 to 7 1/2 feet in length (in a medium- to medium-light action with a moderate rate of flex). My choice is Quantum's 7 1/2-foot American Series Bill Dance Crankin' Rod. As stated before, the slower taper flexes allowing the fish to inhale the bait inside its mouth without "feeling" the rod or fisherman. Remember the stiffer graphite rods will actually recover too fast and pull the crankbait from the fish. The lighter fiberglass rods will "give" to the fish, improving your strike-catch ratio. The bottom third of the rod should contain enough backbone for casting distance and fish control. Slower-action fiberglass rods give more to the fish during the fight to protect the treble hooks from pulling out. And the more forgiving action allows better fish landing control when you get him up beside the boat.

The kick-out features on the Fat Free Shad really help in making this bait extremely weedless and the straight lip allows for the lure to vertically dive quickly. The flat sides give the bait less resistance on the retrieve, which makes for better and quicker depth control — and a tighter wiggle that creates a frequency that bass are highly attracted to. Like I said earlier, this polycarbonate body has tremendous buoyancy and it is practically indestructible.

Mark Davis and the Classic bass on High Rock Lake certainly found this out. Neither one could resist this lure.

This lure has my signature on one side of it. It has earned my seal of approval. It is an improvement in deep-crankbait fishing.

Where Bass Live

CHAPTER 22

MY FAVORITE STRUCTURE

Most of our big reservoirs, whether highland, midland or lowland lakes, have both river and creek channels that meander across their floors.

The channels I like best are the creek channels found on lowland and midland lakes, because the channel ledges there are more fishable than river channel ledges. This is because they are not as large and the water there is usually more protected when located in coves. Weather permitting, the channels that meander out into the main lake can also be highly productive (as long as the bass are using that particular depth).

I should mention that I also have good success along river channels in the mid and upper sections of these types of lakes.

Channels found in southern lakes and reservoirs are especially outstanding places to fish because they represent the major type of structure. Creek channels aren't particularly productive in deep lakes. In an extremely deep lake like Powell in Utah, creek channels are not a factor because they are all too deep and inaccessible.

In a large lowland reservoir like Lake Murray in South Carolina or Toledo Bend, Rayburn and Palestine in Texas, coves stretch for 2 to 4 miles with water from 5 to 25 feet deep. The creeks have very little slope to them. And their channels are located at about the right depth.

Channels (especially creek channels) can be red hot in the summer and winter months. Bass use them as migration routes to go deeper and deeper during the temperature extremes. Creek channels are also super spots in farm ponds and mill pounds, which are fed by creeks. Ponds that were formed by creeks that have been dammed should be viewed as miniature impoundments — and the same channel principles hold true with them.

Inside and (especially) outside bends in the channels are one of the most consistent places to fish. My good friend and tournament

Top pros Bernie Schultz (left) and Shaw Grigsby plant part of their own bass condominium on the edge of a creek channel.

legend Roland Martin believes that "90 percent of the time when you find bass in a creek channel, they will be on the bends."

One reason for that fact is that creek channel bends are a little bit shallower than the straight stretches. Explanation: before the lake was impounded, high water washed up over the bank at the bends during the flooded conditions, depositing sand, mud and debris there. This made the bends sort of like small bluffs. Many of these bends are found in the Tennessee Valley Authority chain of lakes.

These places are another example of an irregular feature. And we all know how much bass stack up along any unusual feature in the bottom contour.

With their small bluff-like banks, outside bends have the shallowest water right next to the deepest water. This means that the greatest depth contrast will be located on the outside bends.

When scouting for channel hot spots, look for the most irregular feature on that creek or river. It could be a bridge or tree lying across the creek, a brushpile, cluster of stumps, a big boulder or an old fence row. A bridge would be shown on a contour map, but any natural obstruction will likely not be noted. A logjam in the bend of a creek might be imbedded in the mud, but you won't find it on a map. Another example: when a farmer has a ravine, he often dumps rocks and logs there that have been cleared from his land.

All creek channels have some type of unusual feature that attracts bass. Consider all of the possibilities. The channel might have an old car body in it. That is a good place to fish and it occurs more than you might think.

Any of these places — man-made or natural — provide structure on structure that is the key to finding concentrations of largemouths.

Isolation can also be an important element in locating channel bass. Fish the most isolated cover and structure you can find. This could be an old, forgotten stump or a single brushpile planted by an enterprising angler.

Another suggestion about isolation: if you are in an area where the creek has two or three branches, splits or bends, this area is usually not as productive as stretches with one bend and no branches. Too much cover of the same type tends to scatter the bass out. In that way, channels are no different than abundant rocks, stumps or weeds.

One of the strategies that has worked for me is studying my depthfinder to get a total picture of a portion of the lake or channel. I concentrate on a single section until I can just about identify every type of cover, bottom and creek bend, as well as single (even isolated) pieces of structure. This gives you several possible patterns and the flexibility to track down resident bass on almost any given day.

While studying channels in older reservoirs, you will often find places where the mud, sand and silt have filled in much of the area. Particularly in the creek bends, there will still be some sections with good vertical drop-offs that have not been silted in. Regardless of the amount of siltation, these sharp drop-offs into deep water will never fill in completely.

These places will usually be small. And the fewer you find, the more productive they are. They are more isolated and unusual and offer a greater contrast than the surrounding lake bottom. So they often hold bigger concentrations of bass. These are prime to vertically jig in the summer and winter with a lead spoon.

Where I begin my search for channel bass depends heavily on the time of year, the water clarity, and water temperature.

During early spring, when the channel coves begin to warm into the low to mid 50-degree range and the water clarity becomes semi-clear to clear, I start looking for bass along the channels in a depth of 10 to 15 feet, especially where the creek forms an irregular feature — like a junction, a U-shaped bend or S-bend, along the channel. As the water continues to warm in the days and weeks to come, the small pockets in the creek coves seem to produce well (especially if there is a ditch leading into it). And the last 50 to 100 yards in the rear of the creek can be good, too. If there is a channel bank, it will be the best choice by far. This usually occurs as the water temperature reaches the low to mid-60s and the bass will usually stay in this area until after they spawn.

Normally, the spawning period will last for several weeks until the water temperature reaches the low to-mid 70's. As late spring approaches, bass begin to group up and move back to the channel ledges. With each passing day, they move a little deeper along the ledges.

By mid-summer, many of these bass have moved from the creek coves out to the mouth of the cover and then on out into the main lake. Here again, the majority will set up housekeeping along the key features of the channel — places like where a saddle is formed, two channels that come together or along the U- or S-bends.

Naturally, finding these underwater hideaways requires a good map, a lot of patience and hard work.

The key to successful structure fishing is establishing a depth pattern and this, too, takes time. But once that magic level is found, it can be reliable for several months. In that case, all the hard work can be very rewarding.

As summer ends and fall rolls around, water temperatures begin to cool down and it becomes a time when pattern fishing can really keep you hopping. During the fall, it's not uncommon to catch good numbers of bass deep — even deeper than where you caught them back in the summer — and you can also catch them in the same areas where you found them in the spring (the tail ends of the major creeks). This is because such areas attract huge schools of shad, and since shad is the preferred diet of bass at this time of year, they will be there in numbers to fatten up before winter arrives.

As the days get shorter and the nights longer, the water chills even more and this serves as a signal to bass to move deeper in search of thinner, warmer layers of water.

As water temperatures drop into the low to mid-40s, most of the bass settle down for a long winter's nap. Their metabolism is slow, but they can still be caught. It is considerably more difficult to get them to bite than in the spring, summer and fall, but they can be caught — provided you fish the right places, which means concentrating along the creek ledges and the beds of the channels.

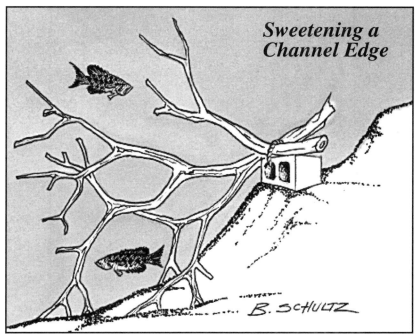

Bernie Schultz

There are few better places to strategically position a brushpile than on the edge of a creek channel.

As I said, fishing this form of structure and establishing a pattern requires concentration and observation. You should carefully think your way through the problem and then, hopefully, come up with a good answer. As you become more familiar with channel fishing, you will begin to recognize these promising spots almost automatically. And because you have full confidence that the bass are there on that particular feature, you are bound to fish it harder and therefore do much better.

The boat dock where I was lucky enough to catch this beauty has everything you could ask for. It is located near the bend of an old creek channel and has a pile of old Christmas trees all around the wooden platform.

CHAPTER 23

FOUR UNIVERSAL BASS STRUCTURES

If you traveled from California to Connecticut and all points in between, you would discover that bass lakes universally have four typical bass-holding structures — boat docks and piers, riprap, boat ramps and duck blinds. These are obvious places that are not fully exploited on most lakes and reservoirs.

These objects are considerably larger, and therefore require some special tactics. In this chapter, we will talk about how and why bass relate to these objects and how they position themselves around them in relation to the sun, shade and current.

BOAT DOCKS AND PIERS

Let's start with the most massive objects —boat docks and piers.

It is a fact of life that certain docks are more productive than others in a lake. One of the reasons that these docks consistently hold fish is that there is a depth change under them. The best are located adjacent to a deep water line, a channel edge or bend. Having deeper water close by gives bass a sense of security and an escape route into deeper depths.

An important element to consider about a dock of this type is not only the depth change, but what is located along that change. To make it perfect, it must have cover and that could be something natural like stumps or it could be man-made (where treetops or other forms of cover were placed around the dock).

One thing I've learned about object-oriented fish like bass, is that it is their instinct to select places that are close to deeper water.

So what makes one dock better than another? Docks and piers built close to a major depth change. It doesn't matter how large the dock is, the important thing is the docks with the rapid depth change in front of them will always be the most productive.

Speaking of cover around a dock, most times it will be man-made. By that I mean, it's where dock owners have sank submerged cover — usually consisting of old Christmas trees, because these type trees (pines and cedars) hold their identity longer than most trees. Many dock owners gather these trees just after Christmas and sink them around their docks. However, other forms of attractors like old tires or stake beds will also work.

When moving in to fish a dock, be sure to take the time necessary to get yourself in the best position to cover the key areas of the dock first. Often, your first cast will be your most productive one. Try to place your cast as close to the dock as possible and then begin working it out to find the cover. Normally the cover in front of the dock will be positioned farther out.

The position of your boat while fishing a dock is of critical importance. When the wind is blowing, it is always best to position the bow of your boat into the wind. This will allow you to fish the area much more carefully and much slower. By drifting with the wind, it will cause you to fish the area much faster and you will not be able to cover the areas the proper way. Plus you will be banging into the pilings and pier posts and spooking catchable bass.

Boat dock fishing will usually be productive year-round. But the ideal times for this type fishing is usually during late spring, summer and early to mid-fall.

My No. 1 choice in a dock would be one that is built close to deep water, has night lights and pole holders on it (which indicate there should be placed cover around it). It would have a breakline running up under it — providing a shallow feeding area, as well as a deep-water escape route. An important note about the deep-water largemouths is that they don't have far to move on a major weather change. They simply drop down into the deeper depths on pressure changes and remain there until the change stabilizes. The fish then move a short distance back to the shallower cover.

To confirm the fact that planted cover is present that you can't see, your depthfinder will show you the size, depth and location of the cover.

If you have never tried this form of fishing, take my word for it, you've missed some great fishing. Boat docks provide great cover and can produce virtually all of the time, and during any season. Give one a try and see if you don't agree.

OVERLOOKED BOAT RAMPS

Believe it or not, most anglers actually drive over one of the best bass holding structures around every time they launch their boat — boat ramps, one of the best and most overlooked bass-holding structures of all.

If you have never fished ramps, I have a few suggestions that may very well open your eyes to an entirely new mode of fishing.

The typical boat ramp is made of concrete, stretches well out into the lake and slopes downward (establishing a clear pathway from deeper water to shallow). If the reservoir ramp is undergoing a typical winter drawdown, you can safely bet that the ramp extends from 5 to 25 feet or more in depth. Also, on either side of the ramp, you will find chunk-rock riprap stretching out along the edge of the concrete into deeper depths. Ramps are made of rough concrete and the rocks around them are rough, too.

Sunlight encourages the growth of algae on the hard, rough surfaces of the rocks and the ramp. To a bass fisherman, this means that a boat ramp is an ideal fishing spot. Bass utilize launch ramps because baitfish habitually use them. Baitfish like shad and minnows feed on the algae and the bass follow to feed on the bait. Also, crawfish use the cubby holes in the riprap, and as we all know, these creatures may be the largemouth's favorite meal of all.

Over the years, bass have learned from experience that boat ramps are frequented by a variety of forage species and these structures provide an easy meal.

The actual boat ramp itself represents a hard clean bottom structure on which there is no cover that the baitfish can use to hide. So when schools of shad are cruising along and around the ramp, they are easy pickings for predator bass.

Most anglers associate night fishing with the heat of summer. Bass fishing at night can be very productive from late spring to early fall and a well-lit launch ramp can be one of the finest structures to fish at night. Lights not only make it easier for the fisherman to see, but they also attract large numbers of baitfish.

I think the best times of the year to fish ramps are during mid-spring (especially late in the day and just after dark), at night during the summer and in the early fall.

Speaking of spring, let me explain something. Although bass are attracted to hard-bottom areas in the spring — and a ramp is certainly a hard-bottom area — I don't believe this attraction is due to the bass' spawning ritual. It is primarily a feeding response learned by the bass. Also, as spring progresses, the ramp and the riprap holds a tremendous amount of heat after being warmed by the sun all day. Bass will be attracted to this warmer water during this time of year. And after the sun has set, the ramp and rocks will still keep the surrounding waters a few degrees warmer through part of the night. You can be sure that bass take advantage of this fact.

Ramps located in calm areas, like in protected coves and creeks, will hold their heat far longer than those located in open water. This is because they are protected from the winds that normally mix and circulate the water in more open main-lake areas. To

***This is the kind of bass that will never be caught by anglers
who launch their boat and roar away from the ramp.***

really capitalize on the warming effects of a ramp, look for protected
ramps on the north side of the lake. These ramps receive more sun
exposure and are warmer than other areas out of the main lake.

While bass follow the baitfish in search of an easy meal, the
light color of the concrete ramp (and the near-white color of the
limestone riprap and concrete) provides a perfect background for the
bass' night feeding forays. In essence, the bass feed very effectively
by silhouetting the baitfish against the light-colored background.

When it comes to lures for this type of structure, your bait
selection can be very broad. Many different lures will work and it
pays to be very versatile. Keep in mind that if the water is murky or
muddy, most of your action should occur along the shallower
sections of the structure. I've enjoyed more success, however, when
concentrating my efforts along the deeper reaches of the ramp and
associated structure. This is particularly true in clear water areas in
late winter and early spring.

I'm sure that many of you are asking, "Doesn't all the traffic
around the launch ramp spook the fish?" Well, only to a degree.

Sure, bass holding in shallow water may be spooked by heavy traffic. The thing that you have to remember is that ramps are areas habitually used by the bass and they grow accustomed to the usual flows of traffic over their heads. This must be true, because I've caught fish on boat ramps regularly throughout the day all year long — even when the ramps were in heavy use.

From the fish's perspective, I suppose it's like learning to sleep after a railroad has been built right behind your house. The first few trains might wake you up, but eventually you learn to snooze right through all the commotion.

Whether you are fishing launch ramps by the light of the sun or under the purple-glow of a blacklight at night, boat ramps are one of my most productive honey holes. Give them a shot, because they may very well become one of your favorite fishing spots, too.

SOLVING THE RIPRAP RIDDLE

Another great bass fishing area is a long section of riprap.

Riprap is broken rock walls or levees that help to hold back the water along the sides of a dam or where a roadway, railroad or bridge crosses a lake. They are designed to prevent erosion and are excellent places to fish.

Maybe I should rephrase that last part about excellent places to fish and emphasize that only certain areas along a riprap are excellent places to fish. It all may look the same above the surface, but it is beneath the surface that counts. It's important to learn as much as possible about what you can't see, and this calls for a good map and depthfinder. Search for any unusual or irregular features. You are subject to catch a single bass anywhere along a riprap, but both the bigger bass and concentrations of bass will usually be relating to some irregular feature.

Here are some examples:

On some Army Corp of Engineers reservoirs, you will see a spillway intake and naturally think that this is where the main river channel feeds the dam. This is true in some cases, but not in others. Instead, the channel reaches the dam at a different point and stops. The location of the inlet and outlet works in a dam is determined by such factors as discharge hydrology, soil, geology and so on. And each dam is constructed individually.

There are, however, several rules of thumb. If the axis of the dam is in a relatively wide flood plain, it is desirable to locate the outlet structure (spillway) adjacent to a bluff or hill line, so there are undisturbed areas to tie the structure into. If the flood plain at the dam axis is narrow, the outlet work could be located anywhere. Beyond these general rules, local conditions will determine location of the structures.

On many lakes, a small ditch or creek may also hit the riprap and stop. These are key areas to fish on this riprap. Other key areas are anywhere a bridge crosses a channel or where a culvert is installed from one side of the riprap to the other. Sometimes this is visible and sometimes it's not. As stated earlier, a depthfinder or map will pinpoint these hot spots for you. Another way is to watch carefully for currents. On calm days, especially, you can spot water moving towards the submerged culvert.

Another excellent place for bass to hold is where a channel comes in close to the riprap. I've found this situation many times and it has usually paid off.

Roped-off areas to the dam or spillway are also good. Fish both sides of these areas. They are as close to the main flow as you can get and, while they usually won't be as good as the intake itself, schools of bass or single fish will move in and out periodically.

You will find this configuration quite often, especially on highway riprap where the roadway crosses a creek or a portion of the lake. Most maps will show these highly productive, irregular spots on a riprap wall. The key areas could be where the small channel hits the rock wall and where it leaves the riprap on the opposite side. The best area to fish is 50 yards on either side of the ditch.

A real gold mine on reservoirs is anywhere that a new railroad was built after the lake was formed. Naturally, the old track is submerged. If the old track is close enough to the new one, it can be a super fishing area. There is usually riprap rock along the new tram as well as the top of the submerged one. Both can be excellent to fish, depending on the depth the bass are using and just how deep the old tram is. Some fish can be caught almost anywhere along it, but to save fishing time, concentrate on the key spots. The same example would apply to an old and new highway crossing a lake. There will be riprap along the new road, while the old submerged highway probably will be concrete, slab or asphalt. Still, it should produce plenty of fish.

Other good key features often found along or near sections of riprap include points, submerged rock piles, or some form of submerged cover like a big tree top, log jam or stump field.

Most lures will work just fine when fishing riprap, but one thing to keep in mind when using "feel" baits like a grub, jig-and-pork and plastic worm is to use the lightest leadheads and sinkers you can. Heavier ones drop quicker and fall between the cracks and openings between the rocks. Lighter weights do two things: they make baits fall slower and they are less likely to hang up.

I've had great success fishing this form of real estate and you can, too.

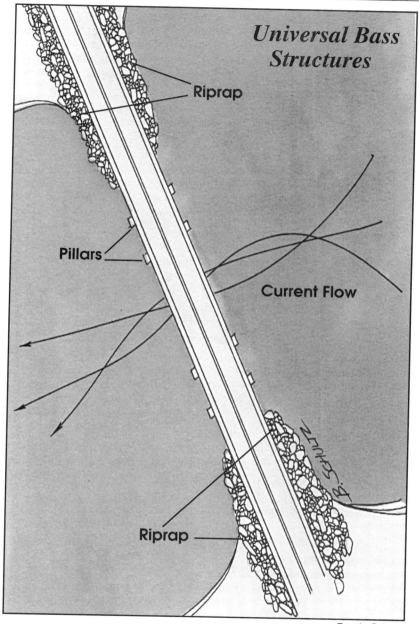

Bernie Schultz

Highway bridge riprap — along with the numerous pillars — can be excellent places to fish. The key with riprap is to find some unusual feature that sets it apart from the rest of the rocky structure.

DUCK BLINDS

When bass are shallow, wooden duck blinds can really be good, simply because they provide cover and shade all day long — forage fish like shad will be attracted to it, too. On large reservoirs and big lakes, duck blinds are usually positioned on points or out in major flats. On large shallow flats, these objects are prime bass cover.

There are important factors to consider when fishing blinds.

The first is boat position. The direction the water is moving and the position of the sun are the next considerations and the two factors determine where the bass will be positioned.

Boat positioning is critical when fishing a blind. It is always smart to take the time to position your boat where you can make an accurate cast without running the risk of hanging your lure and ruining the spot when you go to free your bait. By making accurate casts, you will be able to cover 100 percent of the potential strike zone. When the wind is blowing, this is even more critical.

Keep in mind that largemouths can sometimes be caught at any spot around a blind. But there are key locations that are best. The direction of moving water and the direction of the sun will determine if these conditions exist.

There are four forms of current — wind current, current being pulled through a dam or over a spillway, tidal current and river or creek current. In all of these situations, the effect on fish is the same. Determine the direction of the water flow and most of the time the bass will be in the shade facing the current (on the up-current side of the blind). During low-light hours, bass may not hold as tightly to the cover as they will at other times.

They may roam as much as 15 to 20 feet from the blind, but if a strong wind is blowing against the object — regardless of how cloudy it may be — bass will hold very tight (the same as they do on bright sunny days).

What makes one blind hold more bass than another one? There are several things: the size of the blind, the amount of cover and shade it provides, the location, depth of water (both under it and nearby) and the type of bottom beneath it. Blinds can be very productive if they are fished correctly.

I've often been asked how much time should you spend fishing a single duck blind. Well, first you need to forget about watching the clock. When fishing any object, regardless of size, confidence is the key— not time. The second you lose confidence in a spot, it is time to move on to the next one. If you don't have confidence, you will be going through the motions, while lacking the concentration and thought that should be behind your technique.

CHAPTER 24

POINTS POINT OUT BASS

I can't tell you when the first bass fishermen realized that most bass spend a major portion of their adult lives in open, deeper water areas. Possibly, that discovery was more by accident than by design. But either way, in the past century the technique of bass fishing that we call "structure" has gained serious credibility.

Today, structure fishing is the modern bass angler's cornerstone of success. With the ability to locate structure comes a better knowledge of the black bass — its habits and habitat.

Consider that many of the large reservoirs across our country offer miles and miles of shoreline and thousands of acres of open water. They are a lot different from the little pond out behind the barn where you can cover every foot of the shoreline twice each evening.

To find bass on big water, you have to know where they are most likely to be and then concentrate your efforts only on spots that offer the greatest promise. You won't be right every time out, but the odds will be tipped heavily in your favor.

Of all the different types of structure a lake offers, one of my favorite bass hangouts is a point.

Many bass anglers rely on the saying "points point out fish." And on most lakes, that is true. The configuration of many points can be determined by studying the terrain visible above water. Steep hillsides and bluffs often indicate fast falling points, while flatter shorelines usually mean longer, more gentle points. But there are numerous types and some are better than others.

Which type is best? Well, if you were to limit an experienced structure fisherman to one type of underwater terrain, his first choice would undoubtedly be a creek or river channel that runs in close to a point. These are called channel points and they are usually best.

Let me explain the term "structure" again.

Visualize structure as the floor of the lake, extending from the shallows out to deeper water. More precisely, it is any unusual or irregular features on the lake bottom that are different from the surrounding bottom areas.

Points come in all shapes and sizes, so a good contour map is a necessity.

Structure comes in all shapes and sizes. As I stated before, it can be straight or crooked, contain dents and depressions, or be flat. Some structure is long; some is short. Some is steep, sloping, barren, brushy, grassy, stumpy, rocky or mossy. It can be shallow or deep — on the shoreline or offshore in open water.

One of the best ways to grasp the concept of structure like points is to use your imagination when you are out hunting, or just walking. Look at the surrounding countryside and picture how it would appear if the entire area were inundated with water.

Try picking the key places where bass would most likely hang out. As you do this, you will begin to associate specific types of structure. A map and depthfinder will help. But if you also associate features with those you can see above the ground, it becomes a whole lot easier. Then, the next time you fish a creek bed shouldering into a point, for example, you might be able to compare it to one you saw last fall while hunting.

Anytime a creek channel runs in close to the bank or a point, it is a prime spot. You are not going to find fish there every time, but sooner or later they'll be there. These type of points are always worth checking and if you're going to fish points, it is smart to fish the ones with a channel nearby.

Let's say you have located a school of bass at daybreak on the inside cove end of point. It's a great beginning and you pick up a few fish or even limit out right there.

The next morning you can't wait for the alarm clock to go off and you rush right back to that spot — armed with the same lure and technique as yesterday. But on this morning you draw a blank.

Now is the time to analyze the situation. There could be several reasons why the fish weren't there and you need to determine this. Your first two thoughts would probably be that either the fish have moved or just aren't hitting. These images may pacify the mind, but they aren't going to catch fish for you until you begin to experiment.

It is possible the bass may not prefer yesterday's lure. So you had better get busy trying a variety of other offerings — or maybe it's the retrieve that bothers them. Yesterday, they wanted the lure slowly, so today maybe they want it fast. Maybe they want it with a stop-and-start motion. Maybe they are a little deeper than yesterday, so you may want to adjust for that, too.

When you have gone through the whole routine and still haven't produced results, you have to assume that the fish aren't there. This is smarter than simply throwing in the towel and convincing yourself that they are there, but won't hit. A good contour map can pay off in this situation. If you know the area well, your options become apparent.

You should then assume that the fish have moved from yesterday's spot to another spot along the point. They could very easily be holding at the new spot hitting exactly they way they were yesterday (and falling victim to the same lure and retrieve). If that doesn't work, you go through the routine a second time before you conclude that they may not have moved along the point, but could be hanging around a nearby creek bend. By knowing an area, you always stand a much better chance of catching fish. It's equally important to remember that the bass might not move into the shallower water.

The better you know an area, the more successful you will be. The places where you found fish in the morning could be vacant that afternoon. Generally, bass relating to creek channels will often roam a great deal. They migrate up and down the creek channel (if the depth is fairly consistent).

It is very difficult to find those "underwater highways" I mentioned without a good map and depthfinder or someone showing them to you. The good thing about a map is that it will show you exactly where the channel runs, the channel flat, the channel banks, and the channel points.

Jim Farrior

What Makes a Point Special?

From this bird's eye view, it is easy to see how changes in the lake's bottom contour creates cozy points that attract bass. The underwater points identified above (numbered one through six) are various shapes and sizes, but share a common denominator — they harbor some unusual features that will help draw bass to the spot. In several cases, it is a collection of brush and other wooden debris on the point itself. The attraction of some of these points is their close proximity to a creek or river channel (which provide resident bass with convenient access to deeper water). The closer the channel is to the point, the more productive it should be. The same is true of long points that extend to the actual channel itself.

    It's smart to study your map, select similar spots and give them a try.

    An important thing to remember is that when you establish a terrain and depth pattern, a map will save you lots of time in looking for another channel point in the same area. And if one point like this is holding bass, others in the area could be, too.

As an example, let's imagine a cove with six different points. It is possible that a fish could be on any one of the points, but why waste a lot of time fishing all of them. Instead, maximize your fishing time. Fish only those points with a creek channel nearby. Without question, these will be best. Determine which points are located where the channel moves right by them.

Obviously, I can't promise you a school of bass on every one of the places we've discussed, but I can promise you this — if you will fish enough of them, you will acquire a tremendous amount of valuable experience. And sooner or later, you will find a real bonanza on that bit of structure we call a channel point.

This big female bass had been living under a jumble of timber lodged in the bend of a small creek in a wetlands system in west Tennessee. A slow-moving jig got her attention.

CHAPTER 25

WETLANDS CHANNEL BASS

Wetlands are not noted for surrendering big bass, but they are known for good numbers of respectable-sized fish. The wetland largemouth homes are most renowned for their unmatched scenery.

Wetlands are area covered by either ground or surface water. They are covered by water for at least a portion of the year (the depth and duration depends on rainfall amounts). Some are covered with water throughout the year. These places, also called swamps, sloughs, marshes and potholes, are home to a variety of vegetation and a major part of our ecosystem.

I'm partial to fishing wetlands, especially during the late fall. Let me share with you why I love this type of bass habitat.

Typically, the water elevations are lowest and water clarity is at its best at this time of the year. Water temperatures are cooling down and much of the submerged vegetation is dying off. All of these factors help move the fish closer to the channel banks — making them easier to find and catch.

One of the best lures I've ever used in this situation is Strike King's new rattling version Bootlegger Jig, spiced with a junior-sized Bo-Hawg frog. This jig has a Diamond Dust head and Mirage skirt for more reflection. It comes equipped with a big-bite 4/0 Eagle Claw Lazer sharp hook that has a 60-degree angled hook-eye for better hooksets and penetration.

A common approach is to cast from the channel that works its way through flooded bottomland to the channel bank. Here, the bass have all they need — plenty of cover and deeper water close by. Working a lure like a rubber-skirted jig requires a very slow presentation since we are fishing from deep to shallow. Move the jig too much, and you will likely miss perhaps the most productive spot along the ledge — the place where it drops off the quickest. So

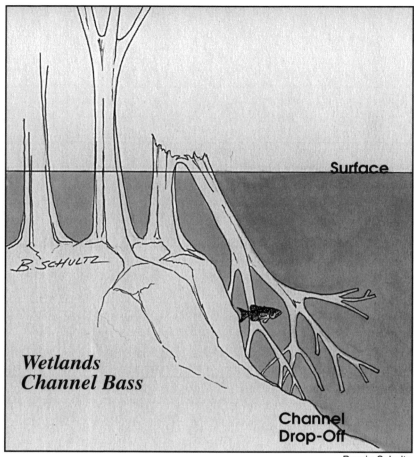

*Wetlands
Channel Bass*

Surface

Channel
Drop-Off

B. SCHULTZ

Bernie Schultz

***Whenever you find submerged cover down in the channel —
like a log or treetop — it's almost an automatic hot spot.***

moving the rod tip 2 feet can and will pull the jig too much (as well
as off the ledge into the channel). You will often catch many of your
fish right up against the vertical bank itself.

Whenever there is submerged cover down in the channel —
like a log or treetop in a depth of 5 to 8 feet — it's almost an automatic hot spot. Bass love it, especially if the cover is around a bend,
a submerged ditch, sharp drop-off or vertical bank. It is always smart
to watch for any changes in the treeline. By doing this, you will be
able to detect deeper areas along the channel bank.

For example, brush along the bank usually indicates a much
shallower bank. But if you see hardwoods like cypress trees, this can

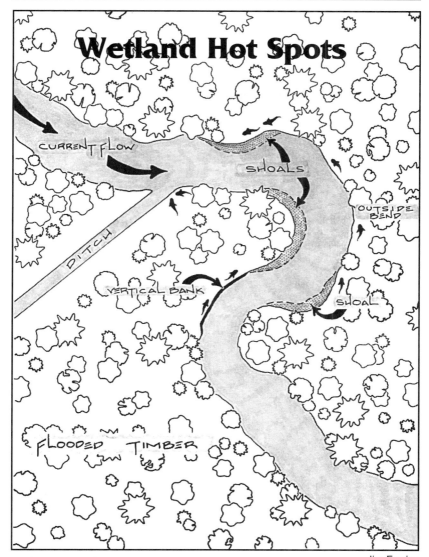

Jim Farrior

The Roadmap to Bass

From this overhead view of a channel slicing through a flooded wetland forest, we can see the type of places that are especially attractive to bass. Any channel that penetrates a field of flooded timber is attractive; but the presence of secondary structure like a shoal, verticle bank or outside bend puts largemouths in predictable spots.

indicate deeper water. Notice that I said "deeper water," not deep water. Three feet is deeper than 2 feet, but 3 feet is not deep. It is these changes in contour that attract bass.

When fishing wood, start by using the best equipment. That starts with the proper rod and action. Baitcasting is best because it provides more power than spinning for this form of real estate. The action should be fast with a sensitive tip and plenty of backbone for a good hookset and to move a fish out of the cover into open water. I prefer a Quantum Bill Dance American Series 6-foot rod or longer over a 5- to 5 1/2-footer simply because it gives me much better control of a hooked bass. Plus, the longer rod provides for a stronger hookset, helps quickly erase any slack and reduces line stretch instantly. Also, the longer pole will help to keep your line tight during the fight.

It is difficult to predict the exact moment when strikes occur. The majority of the strikes will happen when the bait leaves the last section of cover — unless you are jigging it up and down in one place. If that's the case, the strike could take place at any time.

When casting into the timber and the submerged cover, work the jig-and-pork combination steadily, smoothly and slowly. As the lure clears the branches, remember to slightly lift or stall the lure and then sweep it slowly ahead before a controlled drop begins. Also, with this type of fishing, it is important to check your line for any frays or rough spots. If you feel any abrasion, re-tie. I normally re-tie every 30 minutes or so regardless of whether I feel a rough spot or not.

Let's talk about the places on these little waterways where most of the bass are usually located. The most productive areas are those very close to the deepest water — along the submerged banks in an outside bends of both the slough and main channel. This is where you will usually find the deepest water. The bass holding in this location may be positioned just below the upcurrent shoal, around the bend or just above the lower shoal (where the water usually begins to shallow somewhat).

Another key spot is where small ditches or creeks enter the wetlands channel. Here, largemouths will normally position them-selves on the lower point — especially if there is a current present — and any area along a vertical bank with deeper cover, like logs, limbs or treetops.

As I said earlier, I'm kind of partial to places like these. And I'll just bet that if you give one of these wetland areas a try, you will agree with me.

CHAPTER 26

A SHALLOW APPROACH

One of the greatest aspects of bass fishing is the variety of ways and styles it offers the American angler. Bass fishermen can spend a day walking the bank of a farm pond, wading a small creek or fishing an old river slough in a johnboat. Or they can speed across the surface in a fancy bass boat using the latest electronic equipment, trying to locate deep structure and that honey hole that's holding a school of bass in one of several hundred big reservoirs that are found throughout the country.

This is what makes bass fishing so special. The unlimited number of ways there are to catch bass.

I think most bass fishermen prefer the more laid-back shallow-water approach, which I often take with some of the many river sloughs located in the Mississippi river bottoms (between St. Louis and Baton Rouge).

This type of fishing involves casting to objects of shallow cover in a depth of 12 to 18 inches of water. And one lure that is tailor-made for this type of situation is the spinnerbait. It is an ideal bait when you have normal river conditions like extremely shallow, murky water that is laced with many different forms of wooded cover. That wooded cover consists of stumps, logs, treetops and standing timber, for the most part.

One of my favorite spinnerbaits for this type of fishing is a 1/4-ounce Strike King Spin-Dance that is spiced with pigtail pork trailer that not only adds buoyancy for these shallow conditions, but additional tail-action, (giving the lure more eye appeal) as well.

In fashioning a spinnerbait for these shallow situations, I usually stay within the 1/4- to 3/8-ounce range and prefer different blade choices dictated by the water conditions. In fairly clear water, I use double blades with light color patterns. For muddy water, I switch to a single-bladed spinnerbait in the darker colors.

Without question, the popularity of these lures is well deserved. These baits enable a fisherman to work many forms of cover without having to worry about hanging up every 6 to 8 feet during the retrieve. It is the type bait that can be fished in, through,

My friend and fishing buddy Ray Hobbs of Wal-Mart knows that the Scout is a great crankbait for shallow cover.

over and around most types of cover. Yet, when visibility is extremely good, the largemouth will not normally follow a spinnerbait as far as they will follow plastic worms, plugs or jigs. Spinnerbaits, for the most part, are most effective in murky water on individual bass rather than groups of bass.

Spinnerbaits are super lures when loner largemouth are holding tight to cover. These bass make their living by responding quickly to prey that comes close to their holding territory. They respond much like a smallmouth in fast water that must decide quickly whether to strike before a meal is swept away by the current.

Bass that respond to spinnerbaits are normally reacting to the sudden appearance of the flashing object, the vibration of the blade and the enticing wiggle of the skirt and pork when they have approached the lure. These fish do not have the opportunity to size up or line up the lure before striking. They strike from any position, so they may be coming at the lure from an awkward angle. The outcome is that sometimes they don't become securely hooked. When this occurs, most fishermen often sense that the bass is short striking.

Speaking of short strikes, if this should start to occur, a smart solution is to add a so-called trailer or stinger hook to the main hook of the spinnerbait (but only if the cover will allow it). The large eye of this second hook is slipped over the barb of the main hook and the trailer is held on by one or two small rubber or plastic washers.

The system works, but it is primarily because a bass attacking suddenly from an awkward angle has less chance of missing two hooks. It is best to use a trailer when the terrain will permit and in open areas. When you are fishing only the side of cover, you can reverse the second hook to improve your catches even more.

Here's something you might find interesting and helpful the next time you are faced with murky/muddy conditions. You will be amazed at just how shallow bass will be when the water turns yucky — off-colored, stained, murky or muddy. The key reason that they move so shallow is simple: they can see better. There is more light penetration in 1 foot of water than 2 feet of water and we all know that a bass is a sight-feeder.

Although bass are primarily sight-feeders, they will call upon other senses for input when feeding. The lateral lines are sensory organs that pick up vibrations. And the fish's sense of smell is surprisingly refined. This is why it is best to use a fish attractant on your lure.

Anytime you are fishing murky to muddy water always try to fish objects — simply because bass become very object-oriented and zero in on shallow cover. Another tip is to fish tight as possible to objects. Making several casts to each object is another smart move. Also, work your lure closely to the surface and as slowly as possible.

I once read where a writer remarked that "What a spinnerbait is suppose to look like is anybody's guess." He also said that it looks like nothing a bass would normally consume, meaning it looks nothing like natural forage. Well, I disagree with that. We all know that a jig is a high-percentage lure that resembles many different forms of forage. A white jig swimming through the water looks like a shad or minnow; a brown jig bounced on the bottom looks like a crawfish.

If you place a spinner above the so-called-looking "jig", it looks like a shad or minnow swimming under something that flashes and vibrates. And it helps hold it up by allowing it to swim at a constant depth level (depending upon your retrieve).

So I do feel it looks like something in the food chain.

It sure looks more like living forage than some lures on the market that are supposed to represent something a bass usually eats. That is my opinion, for whatever it's worth.

Another great lure for the times when the bass are shallow is a Strike King Scout crankbait. A crankbait might sound like an unusual choice for shallow situations, but this is one diving bait that can really work over skinny-water conditions.

For example, let's say that we are fishing shallow from 6 inches to 2 feet, but the bass are suspended from 1 to 3 feet deep over 3 to 6 feet of water. In this case, the lure I would tie would be the small Scout plug, which will dive only a couple of feet on a long cast. It's got a great little wiggle and is without question the most weedless shallow-running crankbait I've ever fished. This little bait is tailor-made for weedy and brushy cover. You can run it, stop it, dart it and even float it. You can fish it as fast or as slowly as you want to — keeping it at all times in the strike zone of the shallow, suspended bass.

Since the Scout crankbait has a fantastic built-in wiggle it is always best to tie directly to the 0-ring on its nose. Never use a heavy leader or swivel as they will restrict the plug's wiggle and action.

With the Scout and shallow cover, I always try to keep the lure in the strike zone as long as possible by casting parallel to the structure or cover. For example, work the shaded side of a log first and cast parallel to the log, so that you can retrieve the lure along the length of the wood. If you cast perpendicular to the log, your lure will be in the strike zone only a fraction of the time. Instead of covering 100 percent of the log, you will only be covering approximately 5 percent.

Another thing I do when fishing shallow cover of this type with a lure like a spinnerbait or the Scout is to use a heavier weight line. It is not uncommon for a bass to dive down into the cover after striking the bait and hang you up. With a heavier weight line and a fast-action rod, you can horse the fish easier and bring it into open water. My choice in line is a 30-pound test weight. That's right — 30-pound, but the 30-pound I'm using has an outside diameter of about 17-pound test line. It's called MagnaThin, and is extremely strong line with low stretch of a very small diameter.

You know, if you fish a bait like this enough, you're going to discover that these little shallow diving plugs are among the best possible tools for covering a lot of water and finding fish. If you have an excellent pattern, the correct color of the lure and the right cover to fish, you can cover more water with one of these crankbaits than you can with a spinnerbait. That's because you can throw it and work it in both cover and open areas — and then retrieve it as slowly or as quickly as the conditions will permit.

In shallow water, I keep the Scout in the strike zone as long as possible by casting parallel to the structure or cover.

You can add versatility to a bait like the Scout in the way you retrieve it. By using a lot of rod tip movement, you will give the lure more action. Snap the rod tip from side to side or up and down as you reel the lure back or try to add an erratic action to the bait. By doing this, you will increase your odds tremendously. This lure can also be effective on top (especially during the warmer months).

My best technique for this situation is to cast the lure out, reel it down quickly just beneath the surface, and then allow it to pop back on top. When fished this way, the Scout dives head-first, but surfaces-tail first. Because the lure floats so well, it can be fished as quickly or as slowly as desired.

One presentation involves cranking the lure down around cover, stopping it and then allowing it float back to the surface. This looks very natural to a predator. An escaping baitfish will normally head for the surface when a bass is pursuing it. A bass has a hard time taking in food with its suction-pump mouth when it's on the surface, because the air the fish engulfs serves to break the sucking action.

We've all had bass blast a crankbait just as it's being lifted from the water or as it begins its upper trajectory at the end of the retrieve. A trailing bass attracted to the lure might suddenly make the decision to strike because the bait is heading to the surface. It is perceived as escape behavior. This also explains why many anglers often catch more and bigger bass when using the stop-and-go re-trieve with lures of this type, rather than a steady retrieve. The stop-and-go is more erratic and therefore, perceived by the bass a more like the action of a living thing.

Let me tell you another important tip with shallow-water object fishing: always take the time to position your boat where you can make the most accurate cast possible. Also, any time there is a current caused by wind or by water being generated downstream, it is best (if possible) to position your boat down current and cast into the wind, bringing your lure with the current.

Here bass will face the flow and can react to your lure much quicker. And this presentation is less likely to scare them. Bringing a bait up on a fish's blind side will spook him many times. Plus drifting with the wind or current will rush your cast and affect your presentation.

Whenever you are fishing for largemouths, try to visualize where and how the bass might be positioned during every single cast and retrieve. This serves several purposes. First, it gives you a more positive attitude and teaches you to love this sport just a little bit more. Secondly, I play a silly little mental game that forces me to think about the bass and how it should be positioned to ambush my lure as it swims by. It also amazes me just how shallow bass can be caught. It makes me note the direction of the wind current, the best fishing location, the best type of cover and why accurate casts are so critical. It also makes me figure out the best lure and proper presenta-tion. And finally, it makes me proud to know that I live in a country that affords me the opportunity to go fishing.

CHAPTER 27

BASS LOVE CATTAILS

Ever wonder why bass like cattails? First of all, bass and cattails go together like french fries and catsup.

Let me tell you why. This form of emergent vegetation produces oxygen; and we all know that oxygen is essential for life. Secondly, cattails provide absolute security for fish. Plus, they attract the bass' food. Cattails also purify the surrounding water. They provide shade and offer an edge to which fish and other living things gravitate. And as fishermen, we are drawn to them — because we know these facts.

Many bass anglers believe that they can flip a jig almost anywhere in an area of cattails and catch fish, but that is not usually the case. Sure, there are bass scattered here and there and you will catch a few at times. But more times than not, when they don't connect, most anglers assume one of two things: either the bass are not there or they are not doing the right thing. More times than not, the fisherman is not doing the right thing.

Cattails are just like any other bass structure in that you have to understand this standing vegetation and work them carefully, thoroughly and correctly to catch largemouths on a consistent basis.

The cattail is a wild plant that grows in swamps and marshes throughout the United States and southern Canada. In some places, cattails cover acres of marshland with their waving, green leaves. The larger cattails grow to a height of 5 to 6 feet and have long, broad leaves. The smaller plants have narrow leaves. Cattail flowers become the long, brown spikes that are sometimes used as decorations. On the Pacific Coast, cattails are known as "tulle-reeds."

In most of the places that I fish, cattails grow in 1 to 3 feet of water and floating bogs. They can be found on high spots in lakes and other forms of shallow structure and provide excellent cover for shallow-water bass.

As good as these forms of aquatic growth are, it is important to understand that most plants use nutrients and sunlight to produce plant material and oxygen during the day. But at night, the process

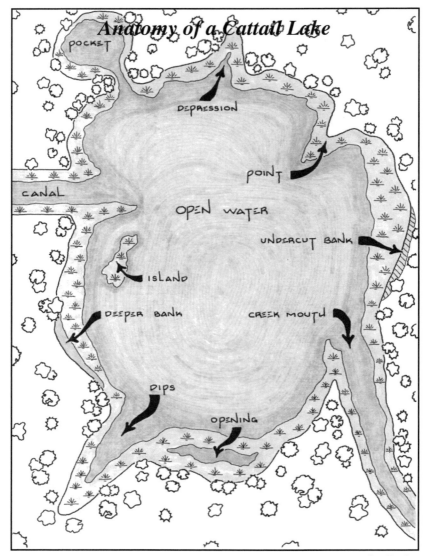

Jim Farrior

***When abundant cattails are the dominant cover in a lake,
look for any irregular feature in the shoreline vegetation.***

reverses and the plant life creates a tremendous demand on the very
oxygen it produced during the day. This alone can have a major
effect on how bass relate to the plants during a 24-hour period.

Over the years, I have found four noticeable times when bass
move away from cattail areas: when the plants turn brown or tan and

begin to decay; at night, especially after a cloudy day; during a heavy bloom, which raises the pH or alkaline base; and after several cloudy, calm days.

These are the times when you will usually find the bass out in front of the cattails. Normally, they will not move a great distance. And when the conditions return to normal, the fish will journey back to the key features.

In this situation, flipping and pitching are high-percentage ways to catch bass that are in a negative feeding mood. You will be able to cover a wider range. Secondly, you will be able to keep your offering in one spot for a longer period of time. Also, you will be able to control the correct presentation every time. And finally, if the bass are inactive, you will be in a much better position to tease them into hitting.

When you approach an area thick with cattails, here are a few key areas to target: dips, depressions, points, pockets, creek mouths, canal openings and deeper banks. Approach a stand of cattails with these facts in mind:

√ Cattail depressions usually have deeper water leading into the mouth of the opening. Both sides (as well as both points) can be productive.

√ Cattail points closest to deeper water are usually the best.

√ Deeper cattail banks are very productive areas, especially around the small pockets and outcroppings that extend out. These spots are sweetened even more when you can find some form of object there (treetop, deeper vegetation, dock or log).

√ When fishing cattails, remember that creek mouths, both points leading in, up to 25 yards on either side of the points and up into the creek itself can all be excellent. The cattails along the creek and canal bank will usually have slightly deeper water around them. Keep in mind that cattails are only as good as the depth around them.

√ Undercut cattail banks are great, but they are usually difficult to locate. Anytime I discover banks with a depth of 3 feet or more, I use a canepole to probe the spot for undercut spots. Once I locate such an area, I then check to see how far it extends down the bank by probing along at several-foot intervals. Of course, I spook some bass in the process, but they will return.

Often, by reading the shoreline you can tell where the deeper bank ends or begins by the change in the land formation or slope.

Undercut cattail banks will hold far more bass than any other cattail bank. I vividly remember bank-fishing a small lake years ago that was completely surrounded by cattails. I soon noticed that only one 25-yard section of the bank produced fish. So, naturally, I became curious about why this stretch of bank was so popular with

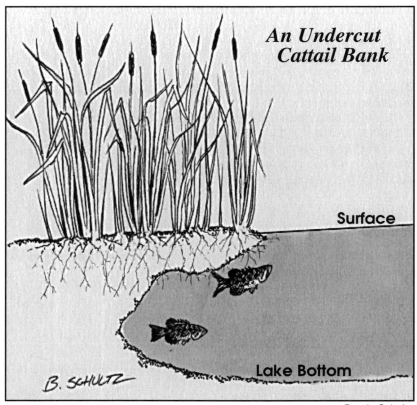

Bernie Schultz

Undercut cattail banks are the best spots, but they are usually difficult to locate. They will hold far more bass than any other cattail bank.

the lake's bass population. As I was preparing to take a closer look at this area, I hung another big fish. But this bass did not head for open water. Instead, it swam backwards towards me and appeared to just keep on going when it reached the very bank I was standing on!

Since then, I have been on the look-out for undercut banks. Sometimes it is a waste of time, but when I get lucky enough to find one, it usually pays off. But remember that it takes time and patience to search out many of the hidden, irregular features found on cattail-laden shorelines. Once you pinpoint these hot spots, though, they will often produce bass repeatedly year after year.

√ Any small opening in a cattail patch could produce a really big fish. Always give it a try if you can reach it with a reasonable cast.

√ A cattail-lined canal can be outstanding. Both sides of the canal are worth checking and there will often be a deeper hole at the mouth of these canals (that can be especially productive during the early and late hours, as well as overcast days).

Keep in mind that a cattail area is only as good as the depth around it. Remember that wind and sun directions are also important considerations.

Sunlight is important in determining which cattail bank to fish. I recommend concentrating on the shady side. During the early morning/late afternoon hours (as well as cloudy days) the bass can be almost anywhere in this vegetation.

It's important to recognize the difference between cattails and bulrushes.

Keep in mind that bulrushes grow much taller than cattails and are usually found in slightly deeper water. Being taller, they cast more shade and are able to grow in deeper water. So bulrushes will usually cover a larger area. When fishing bulrushes, I concentrate on basically the same irregular features as I described with cattails. But I've had considerably more success fishing the bulrushes because there is usually more productive water available to fish. In other words, recognize that bulrushes on a shallow bank will grow out into deep water than cattails — and this creates more fishing area.

In most cases, it is difficult to fish the interior of large areas of bulrushes and cattails that extend very far out from the bank. So it is important to zero in on matted areas, edges, small openings and points along the edges. Also, always fish cattails and bulrushes close to deeper water, as well as all shade lines. The deeper-water areas will attract more bass, while the shady sections tend to hold more fish than the brighter areas. When bass are relating to the brighter areas, they will usually be too far back to reach with a lure.

In contrast, bass in the shady areas will be closer to the edges where you can easily present a bait. The later it gets in the day, the farther the shade line will extend out from the edge.

Plastic worms, spinnerbaits, grubs, rubber-skirted jigs, topwater plugs and crankbaits can be very productive for fishing the edges of this cover (provided that the bottom terrain is conducive to fishing such lures). If there is submergent vegetation out in front of the bulrushes and cattails, your lure selection will be limited.

I'm sure you know that success in bass fishing — like anything else in life — comes from experience. It's not different with cattails and bulrushes. One of the best ways to learn more about this form of fishing is to go and give it a try. This alone will increase your skills and make you more aware of just how productive cattail fishing can be.

CHAPTER 8

THE LILY PAD SURPRISE

The words "bass" and "lily pads" are almost synonymous.

From the time a youngster begins his fishing career, he quickly learns that bass hang out around this form of emergent vegetation waiting for forage to happen by. Pads also provide a tremendous amount of cover and shade, which makes areas of this type even more attractive.

When we speak of pads, most fishermen conjure up an image of beautiful green bonnets lying on the water's surface. But when the water temperature turns cold, lily pads turn brown and die, The bonnets break away from the stems and sink beneath the surface. Are they still productive then? Well, you can bet your most cherished lure that they are.

The dead pads form a canopy which provides a tremendous amount of cover, shade and feed.

As you know, Mother Nature has done what she's done since time began. She's changed the seasons from spring to summer, from summer to fall, and from fall to winter. While lily pads are dead at this time, they still play a large, productive part in the lives of largemouth bass.

It's amazing to me how many fishermen believe that bass just disappear and quit feeding during the dead of winter. It just isn't so. They don't simply disappear and quit feeding. Surprisingly, the largemouth can tolerate one of the widest temperature ranges known to man — from just above the freezing mark to over 90 degrees. They are cold-blooded creatures, so water temperature affects their behavior and metabolism.

Bass are most active when water temperatures range from 65- to 75-degrees. But when temperatures are low (between 40 and 50 degrees), they normally don't move much. Below 40 degrees, the largemouth's activity is very minimal — although, they do continue to feed throughout the winter.

Naturally, energy requirements are low due to their metabolic rate. Therefore, feeding is infrequent. A light meal every four

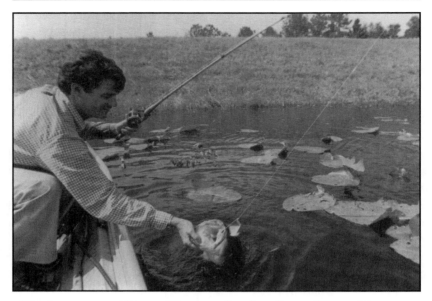

Big-bass expert Doug Hannon lands a huge lily pad bass.

to five days may be all that they need. But this fact doesn't mean you can't catch a few.

I think there are two real keys to catching winter bass. Obviously, you have to locate them and then you have to offer them something that looks and acts extremely natural — a lure you can work at a snail's pace.

My choice is a Strike King Pork-O, a 7 1/4-inch piece of pork that is uniquely cut to give it a natural, realistic swimming action. I don't know of another lure you can work as slowly in this form of cover or one that reacts the way it does. I think the Pork-O represents the next best thing to living prey. It's long and thin, has an appealing profile, and it's silent, so nothing about it presents any-thing negative to tip the fish off that it's an impostor.

When fish aren't feeding actively, it takes quite a bit of extra effort and patience to provoke strikes. And that's where the Pork-O comes in. As I said before, the fact that it is made of pork, just adds something extra to your fishing. Perhaps it's the texture and taste it provides. The texture makes it feel so alive that a bass will try to eat it. As I mentioned earlier, the Pork-O contains salt, which is sodium chloride. Chlorides are a basic component of blood, so a good salty taste definitely tastes like something alive.

Salt is probably the most significant flavor cue that tells bass that it is real food. And this is why they'll hold onto it longer than other artificial lures.

By adding an attractant, an odor trail is emitted as you work the lure through the water. In the sport of bass fishing, pork has a tradition, history and versatility that puts it in a class by itself.

When considering the action of the Pork-O, it reminds me of something I noticed years ago. While fishing the creeks, ponds and small rivers of middle Tennessee, I liked to watch how snakes, mud eels and a few other water creatures swam. Their swimming motion involved the body behind the head. The head is actually tracked in a fairly straight line, while the body undulates up and down or side to side to propel it through the water. To me, another important feature about this bait that attracts bass is that its action really looks natural.

I've found the key to fishing the Pork-O most effectively is to force yourself not to overpower it with a lot of wrist and rod tip action. Moving your rod tip slightly is all that's necessary.

You can easily "overpower" this bait. Moving it too fast will only spoil the natural swimming action. The fisherman who settles on a simple, slow, stop-and-go retrieve will enjoy the greatest success.

Fishing during the winter when water temperatures are in the low 40's requires forcing yourself to be patient and to fish slowly (making several casts to the same area). You have to prepare yourself mentally. In other words, you have to realize that you are probably going to get very few strikes throughout the day. Once you accept that, you will then need to concentrate extra hard to be in a position to take full advantage of those few bites that do come.

Obviously, the dead pads of winter are not the only situation or season when lily pads are worth fishing. Lily pads are universally fine bass cover.

Most natural lakes have lily pads. Some lakes have a large quantity of pads, while others may have only a few restricted patches. A lack of pads in a natural lake usually means there is an over-abundance of hard-bottom areas (which retards their growth).

Bass love pads for several reasons: they provide protection from the sun and overhead predators; create a habitat for minnows, crawfish and other forage in the lake; provide cooler temperatures and more oxygen-rich waters; and pads provide lakes with a certain amount of nutrients, which aids their "respiration" system. The water temperature may be as much as 5 to 10 degrees cooler under lily pads, which is why bass stay shallower in lakes with pads than they do in lakes without such cover.

The absolute best time to take advantage of this prime bass habitat depends on the section of the country you live in. In the South, good pad fishing begins sooner than it does for our northern neighbors.

Florida guide Dan Thurmond with 13 1/2 pounds worth of proof of the value of fishing pads.

I seem to have my best success on cloudy days when the bass tend to hit a lure throughout the day (especially during periods when the barometric pressure is quickly dropping — like just before an approaching storm).

This does not mean that you cannot catch lily pad bass on bright, sunny days. On such days, the most productive times are usually in the early morning and late afternoon. Usually, the later it gets in the afternoon, the better the bass action gets.

I always listen for any sounds of activity in the pads, like bluegills smacking insects, minnows jumping on the surface or any splashes. When you see or hear this activity, you had better get ready because things are getting ready to happen.

Another productive time is when the water is extremely calm or there is a slight ripple on the surface. Too much wind makes it very difficult to fish lily pads efficiently and bass don't usually feed as well.

When it comes to fishing pads, I use a 6-foot (or longer) casting rod that has a fast action and enough strength to horse a bass out of this tough form of cover. It also helps to have 17- to 25-pound test line.

When fishing pads, remember that the No. 1 rule is to get the fish out, up and over the pads — and moving toward you — as quickly as possible. Thick pad patches are no places to play with a bass. Once you get the fish into open water, you can then "play" with it. While horsing the bass, keep your rod tip high and keep your drag tight. If you lower your rod or give the fish line, you will immediately be in trouble.

Keeping in mind that the best catches come when we target specific areas of the pads, choose the lure that best suits the prevailing conditions. Several baits (including topwater plugs, shallow-running crankbaits, spinnerbaits, plastic worms and soft-plastic jerkbaits) can be fished along the edge of a pad bank, but weedless lures (spoons, buzzbaits, floating worms and frogs) are the only choices when the bass are well back inside of this cover.

As with most types of cover, I always search for the key areas where the bass are likely to be. Mother Nature arranges lily pads in all shapes and sizes. Fishing a large section of pads can take the better part of a day because they must be fished slowly and thoroughly. So it makes more sense to concentrate on key areas. You can catch a bass or two by just fishing along the entire rim of a pad field. But your odds increase significantly when you concentrate on key areas. So, don't waste time fishing "look-alike" areas which fail to produce after a cast or two.

Search the pad line for unusual features — like a point in the pads, for example. Make a series of fan-casts across this point and 10 to 15 feet down each side. Then move down the pad line to the next irregular feature you can find.

One thing to look for is any isolated clump of lily pads. Like with any other type of isolated cover, bass using pads will often be attracted to these individual clumps because they are unusual from the surrounding terrain. I have spent an entire day working a large area of pads, only to turn around and catch a limit from a small, isolated patch. Many anglers just don't take the time to move within casting range of these spots. But I no longer pass them up!

Also, don't overlook isolated openings in a field of lily pads. These spots can be difficult to fish unless you work your boat into the edge without making too much noise. A well-placed cast can certainly produce a strike, but getting a hooked bass out through this tangled vegetation can be all but impossible. It's best to carry a stout push-pole, which can be used to reach fished hooked inside of the pads. And this approach is quieter than any trolling motor.

Some final thoughts on fishing lily pads:

√ Carefully position the boat before making each cast. Never make a long, wild cast. It's a good idea to make a series of fan-casts to cover more water systematically and efficiently. Also, plan each cast with full confidence that a strike will occur. Plan a proper, easy retrieve route through the pads. The less you disturb the cover, the fewer bass that will be spooked.

√ Watch for approaching weather changes and plan some pad fishing around them. As I mentioned before, the falling barometric pressure that accompanies weather fronts can really turn the bass on.

√ Don't set the hook too early when a bass strikes. Wait for a second or two after hearing the sound of the "slurp" before reacting. This delay is crucial. Force yourself to pause momentarily before setting the hook — and your hooking percentage will more than double.

√ Keep both the point and cutting edges of your hooks razor-sharp.

And remember, spend most of your time fishing the high-percentage areas — any irregular feature you can find. In the long run, it will save you wasted time and produce a lot more fish.

CHAPTER 29

STALKING OXBOW BASS

Let's talk about fishing some particular spots that produce well for me, especially in the hot summer months when the temperature by midday soars to a scorching 96 to 98 degrees and the humidity is close to 80 percent. There are the hundreds of Mississippi River oxbows that are located from St. Louis to Baton Rouge — and countless oxbows on smaller rivers.

I know it can be miserably hot during this time of year. So why put yourself through all this misery? Well the answer is simple — the dog days of summer are when oxbow bassing is at its best.

One of the challenges of oxbow fishing is the consistently changing water level. For example, on a recent trip, the river had just receded, pulling the water level down to 10 feet. The Mississippi River gauge reading at Memphis a month before registered at 22 feet, and three weeks before that it was over 30 feet. This should give you a pretty good idea of how much water this river run will support.

During the high water times, there is literally miles and miles of flooded water timber and the bass relate to the thousands upon thousands of flooded acres of cover. But when the water is low, they will be relating to structure in the form of sand points, ledges and flats close to deeper water.

A good lure for fishing highly productive, clean shorelines is Strike King's Diamond Shad. The success of a lipless crankbait like this can be attributed to the fact that you can cover a vast amount of cover with it in a short period of time, especially when the fish are relatively shallow. This little bait duplicates one of the predominant forage here — shad. One of the best methods of fishing a lure like this in this type of situation is to fish slow at depths of 2 to 8 feet. Deeper than that usually proves to be nonproductive due to low oxygen levels at this time of year.

How should you fish this bait? Slowly, because the water temperature is almost as hot as the air temperature. A slow, free-falling and yo-yoing type of presentation is always best in this case. Bass can become just as sluggish in hot water as they can in real cold water. This is why you should pay close attention to both presentation and depth.

My old friend Max Baer unhooks a Mississippi oxbow bass.

Another factor that plays a major part in the depth these fish are using is pH. Bass, as well as other fish, are highly sensitive to high parts of alkaline, as well as low parts of acidity. One of the best ways to establish the most productive depth that active bass will be using is to establish a pH breakline. pH is a measurement of acidity and alkalinity in water with 7 to 9 parts most suitable.

Have you ever wondered just how an oxbow is formed? Many of these lakes form naturally as rivers snake their way through the lowland landscapes, cutting new channels, constantly re-routing themselves and leaving behind horseshoe or seascape lakes (where the main river channel once formed a bend). As the lake forms, the river begins to flow through the bend, but in time siltation may partially or completely seal off the old channel — making the lake completely inaccessible by way of the river, except at certain stages.

Oxbow lakes are generally divided into two types, based on their geographic relationship to the river levee. Lakes occurring outside the levee boundary commonly are referred to as landlocked oxbows and are not affected by the river like those inside the levee. In many respects, the two types of oxbows are very different. Normally those outside the levee are laced with cypress trees and those inside the levee are lined with mostly willows.

However, they both share certain characteristics. The most apparent similarity is an abundance of bass. Let me tell you a story about one of my oxbow lakes and how good the fishing can be. Several years ago, I fished 12 half-days during the hottest month of the year. In those 12 half-days, I caught and released 465 bass — and all were taken in less than 2 feet of water.

Catches like those don't happen everyday, but bass are still caught in ample numbers to satisfy even the most pessimistic of anglers. Generally, river lakes like those inside the levee produce more bass, but the landlocked oxbows outside the levee boundaries produce bigger bass. Bass in the 3- to 5- pound class are plentiful in both types of oxbows, but many bass in the 7- to 8-pound class are caught in the landlocked lakes.

Catching fish consistently in either type of oxbow requires a basic knowledge of the river system and how it relates in each type of lake. Oxbows are shallow water lakes and water more than 20 feet deep in the summer is rare. And as stated, bass are caught on shallow water patterns 95-percent of the time. If you were to look at the lake bed without its water, it resembles a large bowl (except that one side where the outside bend of the water once flowed). It is distinctly deeper. And these are the type banks that I like to fish.

At certain times, worms and topwater lures as well as spinnerbaits will be big producers in an oxbow. But no matter what lure a fisherman chooses, there is one factor in river-lake fishing that outweighs everything else — the level of the river itself. In any one year, oxbow fishermen along the Mississippi contend with level changes of 30 feet or more. So each trip to the lake can be completely different and extremely tricky unless you understand fish behavior during rising and falling water. If a bass is to survive in a river-lake, it soon learns in early life to be on the move. Extreme fluctuations are difficult on fish as well as the fisherman. This is why I prefer mid-summer to early fall, because conditions remain fairly stable.

Knowing how oxbows are formed, how each lake relates to the river and how bass relate to the oxbow environment and the

Bill Wolbrecht caught this oxbow bass on a Strike King Diamond Shad lipless crankbait.

changes within it, can be an invaluable aid when planning a trip to an oxbow lake (wherever it's located). This is, however, no substitute for experience. So if at all possible, make your first few trips with someone familiar with these type of lakes. And do not limit yourself to one trip or even one lake. There are hundreds of oxbows and each one potentially holds a trip of a lifetime. And remember, the greatest thrill is not to kill, but let live.

CHAPTER 30

WATERSHED BASS

*S*ome of the best fishing opportunities don't stand out. More often you have to hunt for these special places. You have to search hard and often what you find will surprise you — because these places were right under your nose the entire time.

That's the case with bass fishing in watershed lakes.

These miniature bodies of water dot the countryside of nearly every state, but many anglers usually ignore them in favor of bigger and better publicized lakes. Yet, these little bodies of water can provide unbelievable bass fishing. I personally love to fish watershed lakes. In fact, I've been a long-time fan of them. Watershed lakes are basically easy to pattern and offer exceptional big-bass potential.

They may be small in stature, but watershed lakes are the best that bass fishing has to offer. These type lakes vary in size from less than 5 to up to 1500 acres. But they contain the same array of structure found in the major reservoirs. Submerged humps, islands, channel drops, points, vegetation and timber just to name a few.

It is important to pay attention to the slightest change in depth. A 2- to 3-foot drop in a small watershed lake with an other-wise slick bottom represents a major structure in that lake. Always relate the size and amount of structure to the size of the lake — and never overlook seemingly insignificant structure in these lakes. While these lakes are small, they usually possess the same character-istics as larger lakes.

Most of them are loaded with structure and, like a big body of water, some of the structure will pay off and some won't.

One of my favorite situations is when there is a very shallow flat bottom that extends way out from the shoreline with little or no cover on it. The depth graduates slowly from a foot deep at the bank on out to about 3 feet and then drops off into a shallow ditch that is only 5 to 6 feet deep. Even though that breakline is only about 2 feet deeper than the flat, it is enough to attract and hold largemouths. Another attractive characteristic is isolated stumps that nearly reach the surface. Often they were actually cut down to 2 feet in height before the watershed was impounded.

No doubt about it, watershed lakes make great training grounds for learning more about the habits and habitats of bass. A great many anglers enjoyed their first taste of bass fishing in a small soil conservation lake — either fishing from the shore or a small boat. These little lakes are really great teachers. Because of their small size, they are relatively easy places to establish a pattern on, so the angler can gain the kind of confidence that only comes from catching bass. Bass are usually easy to locate in these lakes. Unfortunately, this also makes them prone to being fished out or having the bass population easily thinned down.

At certain times of the year, one of the main forages in a watershed lake is the crawfish. The reason that bass prefer this little creature is because they are basically easy to catch. And bass dieting on crawfish grow fast due to its protein value. In order to survive, a bass soon learns to measure the amount of energy it expends in relation to the reward received. If a bass must expend more energy than the nourishment, it isn't worth the effort. An interesting fact is that samples of stomach contents from bass taken at various times of the year all across the country tend to support the theory that crawfish alone constitute more than 75 percent of the adult bass' diet in all habitats where crawfish and bass co-exist.

In watershed lakes, I like to use a crawfish-colored crankbait like a Bomber Fat A, as well as a jig-and-pork combination. Both closely imitate a crawfish.

For a lure to be really convincingly effective it first must not only look like the real thing, more importantly it must act like the real thing. Many bass anglers cast and retrieve crawfish-imitation lures in much the same way as they do any other subsurface crankbait, but this is a principle mistake. It is very important that you make it appear to act like a crawfish. It will produce much better if it is worked in a natural presentation — which is slow. Crawfish don't speed along like a shad. They move along at a much slower pace that fishermen should copy.

There are hundreds of watershed lakes that may exist in a single region of one state. The good part is that they provide a lot of variety and can possess many of the same characteristics of big lakes, like points, flats, bluffs, channels, riprap and timber.

The bad part is that you might pick a lake that is past its prime. When fishing these lakes, learn to keep a watchful eye on the bass, their forage and the quality and condition of the water. I can often tell when a lake is out of balance simply by looking at the fish I

J.B. Edwards (left) and Dick Berryman take their aluminum boat in search of big bass in small watershed lakes.

catch. I can quickly tell that something is not right in one of these lakes if I catch a lot of bass that are all the same size (in an older lake) or I catch skinny bass with large heads.

As I stated earlier, there are a lot of good bass produced in watershed lakes — and there are poor ones. Some of the best I've fished are those with a seasonal fluctuation in water levels. With a drawdown of several feet, new plant growth sprouts up along the edges and the shallower portions of the upper reaches of the lake. Moss, grass and minute vegetation appears. Then when the lake level rises during the late spring rains, this new growth provides an excellent forage base for all kinds of life, including bass fry. Tiny microscopic organisms gather on the plants, helping to promote rapid growth of newly hatched bass.

In case you are not familiar with the term "watershed lake," let me define it. It is the land area from which the water drains to a given point. It serves two primary functions — flood control and soil conservation. On land, the water that does not evaporate or soak into the soil usually drains into ditches, creeks or lakes. If the water runs off the land too quickly, it can cut gullies and carry off precious topsoil. And too much water running too fast causes flooding. Channels become choked with sediment and, naturally, carry less water, so the chances of flooding become worse.

To combat those problems, small- to medium-sized dams were constructed on ditches and creeks prone to flooding, slowing the runoff and reducing the amount of eroded soil that is carried with the water. Unlike reservoirs, watershed lakes are disposable and are built to last a rather limited life span, usually 100 years or less. They are designed to fill up with sediment.

Don't ever discount these lakes in your quest for a quality bass fishing experience. While fishing a big impoundment in a big, comfortable bass rig has its benefits, there is something special about fishing these small waters. The thousands of watershed lakes nation-wide offer a vast, often untapped resource to bass enthusiasts. Investigate the potential of watershed lakes and you might just discover that dynamite does come in small packages.

CHAPTER 31

THE BEAUTY OF STANDING TIMBER

When it comes to bass fishing, any good angler can tell you that the name of the game is "cover." And one of the most inviting forms of cover for both bass and bass fishermen is standing timber.

Flooded timber is the type of cover that can keep the average angler busy all day just searching along the floor of these watery forests. To fish standing timber properly, however, and to make the most of the time you have available, you should always have some type of game plan in mind.

During the past 30 to 35 years, the Army Corp of Engineers has created thousands of acres of water where standing timber remains. Here, bass fishing often is at its best, but only if you are fishing the proper lure, depth and location.

Standing timber is such good bass habitat that there are key areas where you just might make 10 casts and catch 10 bass without ever moving your boat.

Humps and ridges are very productive terrain. Bass will move in on top of them and take up stations on these rises above the lake floor. If the ridge has a sharp drop-off, you can expect to find the majority of fish very close to that drop-off. But if it is just a high sloping area, the bass could be anywhere in the area. It is important to remember, however, that they will seek a preferred depth and zero in on the heaviest-cover areas at that depth on the hump or ridge.

One of the quickest ways to find this form of real estate is to take a close look at the standing timber. If the growth is relatively the same age, simply look for trees that are standing higher than the others. Chances are they will appear taller because the lake bottom is higher (and that indicates a high spot in the form of a hump or ridge).

This isn't always true, but it is usually the case. Another tip-off is that along the tops of ridges especially you will find smaller diameter timber — usually pine or other soft wood. That is a good indication that a ridge or high spot exists.

A happy Dick Berryman with his prize caught from a submerged ditch that runs alongside and through a stand of flooded timber.

A boat lane is another prime location. A boat lane is a pathway cut through the timber to make navigation safer and easier. The resulting structure is simply two timber lines running parallel to each other.

Bass will migrate along these timber lines and there are several key areas where they will sometimes school and hold. Other likely spots are channels, sloughs, pockets, roadbeds, boat lane intersections and around fallen trees. These are all good places to fish. Again, I need to emphasize that the preferred depth will determine the best spots at any given time.

Submerged channels running through a stand of timber are one of my favorites. In fact, channels are often the top structure to fish in flooded timber.

Depending on their relationship to the correct depth, the areas that I prefer to fish along channels that extend through timber are: 'U'-shaped bends, 'S' bends, saddles, the two channel ridges, channel junctions and sloughs or depression drains.

Over the years, I've had some fantastic fishing in the areas mentioned. But you need a quality depthfinder and map to help exploit each of these underwater hide-a-ways.

Anytime you can find structure within structure, you have found an excellent area. Examples: a boat dock with a big Christmas tree planted under it; a big stump sitting in the middle of a grass bed; or a log laying next to a bush. That is structure within structure, a term to remember.

Anytime you run across a deadhead or dead-fall, stop and spend time fishing it. Those are fisherman's lingo for a fallen tree that has floated around for quite some period.

At some point, one end of the tree got water-logged and either sank to the bottom, wedged onto some other submerged object or hung up along a ledge, ridge or channel drop. This is an excellent form of cover that can really produce fish for you. It is important to recognize that these objects can be located in many different areas of a lake — not just in areas of standing timber.

You also need to be aware that heavy winds which produce strong currents will shift these trees around until they become dislodged and move or sink (from becoming too water-logged). Consequently, they may not always be in the same place that you found them the last time out.

Any type of deadhead is an excellent place to locate bass, but one that is wedged along a drop-off or ledge is always best. These are the type of objects you should never pass up. Single bass will hang around the exposed end (near the surface), but concentrations of fish will be positioned in the thick cover of the limbs and branches below.

Sometimes a deadhead will position itself in the opposite direction. In this situation, you will usually find fish suspended in the heavier cover located near the surface. This is a great ambush point where predators can attack baitfish as they meander by.

Boat positioning is another critical factor when fishing these objects. If possible, it's always best to make parallel casts to the cover, bringing your lure in the direction that the limbs point.

It is good news for the bass that most fishermen shy away from these areas, because they are often very difficult to fish. Timber

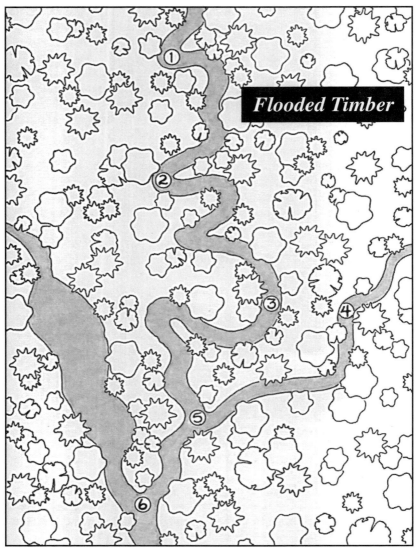

Jim Farrior

Beneath the watery base of fields of flooded timber often lies a serpentine channel with hot spots like bends where the bass tend to congregate.

fishing requires a lot of patience. For many anglers, fishing in the trees brings visions of hang-ups, busted lines and bass wrapped up like Christmas presents in the submerged limbs and cover. Some of these visions are realistic, but if you use the proper equipment, learn a little bit about the terrain, know where the bass are located and then correctly present a carefully selected lure, fishing the timber can be one of the most productive and rewarding methods of fishing.

It might sound as if I'm trying to discourage you from fishing this type of terrain. But truthfully, I am trying to convey that timber is an excellent place to catch lots of bass.

It is very difficult to fish this type of structure without having a hooked largemouth wrap you up in a mass of submerged treetops or around a tree limb. But there can be a positive side to this catastrophe — I have a little trick that will free more than 80 percent of your hung-up fish.

Any time a fisherman hangs a bass up, his first reaction is usually to continue to apply tremendous pressure and reel the fish until he can't reel any more. If he feels any movement or give, he reels in a little bit tighter — until the fish can't swim.

In order to free a bass from this type situation, the fish must be able to swim. When you first feel the fish sound deep into the branches and crochet himself up, keep your rod tip up at about the 2 o'clock position, maintain tension on the fish and then apply the same amount of pressure that it applies to you. For example, if you feel the bass pull down 2 feet, you should counter by pulling back 2 feet. Notice that I said pull back 2 feet, not reel in 2 feet.

The mistake most anglers make is to continue reeling the bass up until they "nose" it up against a limb. When this happens, the fish's mouth is so tight against the cover that it can't swim. Either the line breaks because the fish has the leverage to break it or you will have to break your line yourself — losing both the bass and your lure.

Above the surface, you will see only a percentage of the actual cover. What lies beneath us is the reason you need a rod with lots of backbone and at least 17- to 20-pound test line.

My most productive lures for standing timber include: plastic worms and crankbaits fished along the outside timber edges; a jigging spoon worked vertically; and buzzbaits and topwater plugs during the times when the bass are suspended.

Spend a day or two in the trees and you will share in the excitement of probing standing timber for big bass. Hopefully, the helpful techniques we've discussed will give you an idea of how to approach timber, as well as some inspiration to give it a try.

Fishing the timber is different, very productive, and a tremendous amount of fun.

Whether it is a slow-moving swamp-like lake or a fast-flowing river, I would rather fish moving water than anything else.

CHAPTER 32

MOVING WATER MEMORIES

Over the past 25 years or so, I've really been blessed by being able to make my living doing what I love to do — and that's fish. My job has afforded me the opportunity to travel and fish many different places throughout the United States, as well as Canada and Mexico. But of all the different and exciting types of places — including lowland, midland and highland reservoirs, natural lakes, canyon impoundments, oxbows, sloughs, ponds and swamps — my absolute favorite is moving water.

Maybe that is because I grew up fishing rivers, creeks and streams. Or maybe it is simply the challenge that moving water offers. Possibly it's the scenery and wildlife, along with the constant wondering of what lies just around the next bend. Whatever the reason, moving water is a very special place for me and the reason why countless bass anglers fish the jillions of small moving-water tributaries that America has to offer.

There is something magical about places of this type. I am almost overwhelmed by the power of its life and motion. It never quits calling me to move on upstream or around just one more bend. In these places, you will find fellowship with all kinds of creatures that you seldom see stalking down a brushy, wooded shoreline. In the world of moving water — especially the wilder places — you are in a world of your own.

It's all yours, whether you're there for a few hours or an entire day.

When most anglers think of bass, they seem to overlook the fabulous population of fish that live in our mini-waterways. These super little fisheries provide extremely fertile water, an excellent forage base and plenty of cover and structure that combine to form an ideal habitat for largemouths.

As a general rule, bass are usually considerably easier to locate and catch in places of this type than they are in a big large lake, simply because there is less area to fish.

Think of a creek or river as having three kinds of water: fast, shallow water; in-between water; and slow, deep water. In all of these situations, the current will vary greatly. The largemouth prefers slow or non-current areas, while the Kentucky spotted bass and smallmouth bass prefer the areas that are as close to the fast current as possible (and even right in the flow at times — especially during the warmer water periods).

Like I've said so many times, an angler who can master creek and river fishing techniques (regardless of size) can be an excellent angler on lakes — but not necessarily the other way around. One needs to develop a unique style of boat control, be aware of boating hazards, be able to read the visible shoreline structure (as well as the surface current) and have a keen awareness for lure presentation and control.

It's important to remember that each creek and river — big or small — is going to have its own course, contour, speed, and confirmation. But there is one key feature that is common among creeks and rivers. That key feature is called an eddy, and it is what moving water fishing is all about.

Let me explain that term in case you are not familiar with it.

An eddy is current that runs opposite to the direction of the main flow. It is normally slack water caused by a current break. A current break is an obstruction like a log, stump, piling, dike or land point extending out into the river. Even a hole or depression on the floor of the channel bed can serve as a channel break.

Eddies can move horizontally, vertically, or both. To get a better idea of this, try to visualize a strong current rushing into an object. Water spins out around, over and sometimes downward. It is important to remember that any time flowing water strikes an obstruction, it does two things: it changes speed and direction. Regardless of direction, spinning or swirling water creates either a slow-water zone or slack area.

A horizontal eddy usually forms where the main current flows out and around a point; while a vertical eddy forms where the force of water is pushed upward, after striking an obstruction in the main current flow.

These are the places that are home to many small fish simply because they provide a survival location that attracts the whole food chain. Baitfish and insects are washed from the fast flow into the transitional water and finally into the calmer zones. Gamefish know this and use eddy water as their No. 1 location for feeding. Keep in

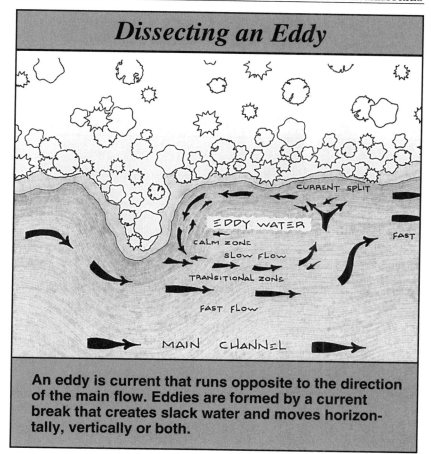

Dissecting an Eddy

CURRENT SPLIT

EDDY WATER

CALM ZONE

SLOW FLOW

FAST

TRANSITIONAL ZONE

FAST FLOW

MAIN CHANNEL

An eddy is current that runs opposite to the direction of the main flow. Eddies are formed by a current break that creates slack water and moves horizontally, vertically or both.

Jim Farrior

mind that all eddies are not going to be productive because some have a reverse current that is too strong.

When you locate an eddy where either a slack or slow current exists, you will usually find that the slackest water occurs in front and in back of almost every obstruction. The same applies for horizontal eddies that form below a point or at a creek mouth.

Normally the front portion is usually best for the most aggressive fish (as long as the water temperature is above 50 degrees). Below 50 degrees, the slack water at the back is best.

Another note of interest is that a slow-water zone that forms on the bottom at the leading edge of an eddy is another great spot for a big largemouth. Also, during the high water times new eddies form and old ones disappear. But when water levels drop, and the current decreases and river or creek levels stabilize, it is not uncommon to

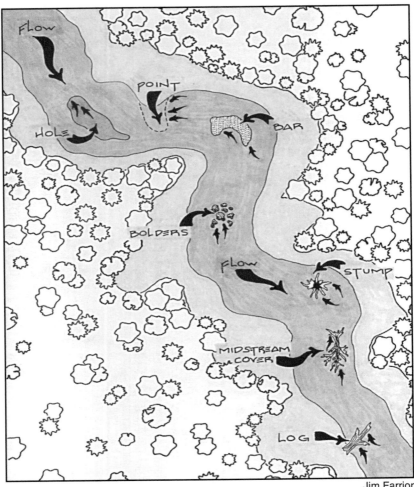

Jim Farrior

With current-laden situations, eliminate water and wasted effort by not spending a lot of time fishing long, straight stretches. Look for key areas like channel bends with cover (like trees, logs and boulders) that has been washed in.

locate bass out along the transitional zone of water — out close to the main-current line.

Eddies are very recognizable for the most part. Look for visible swirls, boils and current flowing in the opposition direction. Floating debris can be a good tip off.

Eddies come in all shapes and sizes — small, large and well-defined. However, others are somewhat more difficult to detect.

There is just something magical about fishing moving water.

Before fishing a creek or river, try to obtain a good quadrangle map of the specific area you are going to fish. One of the best is a 7.5 minute series (topographical) map, which is produced by the U. S. Geological Survey Department. Maps of this type are available for all parts of the country and will show you backroads to the moving-water areas where eddies are likely to form (like bends in the channel and the mouths of creeks) and much more.

Look for key areas. They are often found where the channel bends the most. Don't waste a lot of time fishing long straight stretches. Bends create large current breaks. However, this is not to say that eddies can't be found along the straight-a-ways because they can and should be checked out from season to season. Current speeds that occur during high water periods change the landscape often along these channel banks, creating washes, forming small points and washing down new cover in the form of trees, logs and boulders.

To be sure, there are numerous places along creeks and rivers where bass can be caught, but my favorite are the eddy waters we've just discussed. These are the types of places that I have the most confidence in. It has been my experience that here is where I catch the most fish, year after year.

Learn to recognize and fish eddies and you will improve your success dramatically.

CHAPTER 33

CANAL BASS HIDE IN PLAIN SIGHT

Doing the type of work I do affords me the opportunity to travel and fish some mighty interesting and different places. Some are very productive, others are not. Some are easy to fish, while others are difficult. Some are hard to get to and some are extremely tough to reach. It usually takes a real effort to find the perfect balance. By that, I mean a great fishing place with good access.

There are thousands of fishing holes across America that are virtually untouched, simply because they are hard to get to and places where it is almost impossible to launch a boat into. But if you are willing to work at it, you will usually be highly rewarded.

An example of such a place would be a small canal. Webster's dictionary defines a canal as an artificial water source and these are found in all parts of the country — from Florida to Canada; from California to the Carolinas. Naturally, their basic makeup will vary depending on locale. Some are laced with vegetation, while some with rock and others with wood. But all have similar construction — shallow shorelines with a narrow deeper channel. The key to fishing them is to locate anything irregular in or along the canal.

If you are an angler who enjoys shoreline fishing, you will love canal fishing — simply because the most active bass in this type of environment will be shallow (especially if the water clarity is semi-clear to murky). Clear-water areas are difficult for bass, because of the amount of light penetration. Bass generally have an aversion to light and can see better in shade and darker water (but they won't hesitate to ambush baitfish in well-lite areas). They instinctively associate low light or darkness with safety and for the most part avoid exposure to the rays of the sun.

Bass in clear water behave differently than those in stained or murky water. In clear bodies of water bass are usually found deeper, venturing into the shallows only during low-light times (early or late, on overcast days and when there is a good chop on the water). Both of these conditions cut down on the amount of light penetration, making the fish less wary and, therefore, more active.

What I'm saying here is that given a choice, it's best to select a body of water that has some color if you are planning to fish the middle part of the day.

A minute ago, I spoke of water clarity. Here is a simple way to define what's clear, stained or muddy and how to check the amount of light penetration. Lower a white object like a lure over the side of the boat with a string. At the point where you can no longer see the lure, bring in the string, measure its length — and then double the measurement. The reason we double the measurement is because light must travel down to the object and then return. This will give you the actual depth of light penetration.

Normally, if I can see the lure or object below 4 to 5 feet, I classify that as clear; from 2 to 4 feet, I call that semi-clear; and less than 2 feet is murky.

A typical canal is likely to be laced with wood and other irregular shallow features. It is important to target these places.

Anytime you can find a ditch or drain entering a canal, you have probably found an excellent area. Here, bass will position themselves around the mouth of the drain. If flowing water is present, it is possible to catch 10 bass on 10 casts.

Another key location is a small pocket along the shoreline.

Any place where a canal makes a turn is always an excellent location to catch schooling bass. That is where the water is usually the deepest.

Anytime you see an isolated log, it could be a super object. But take the time to position your boat where you can fish the entire log from the shoreline on out.

It is always smart to be very observant and watch the shoreline for any changes. For example, any spot where the canal banks squeeze in close together could be a dynamite spot — especially if there is a wind current blowing through it. Here, bass will position themselves on the down-current portion to capitalize on the water movement for oxygen as well as forage. This is especially true during the hot months.

In this area that makes up the back end of the canal, bass will herd baitfish into the enclosed section. It's not uncommon to catch several fish here and then be able to return later and catch several more.

Of all the objects found in the water, none seem to excite the confidence of bass fishermen more than exciting looking stumps. If a stump doesn't produce the first time you cast at it, be sure to try it again, again and again.

Any points extending out into the canal will likely be the perfect spot to catch bass (and possibly a bunch of them). Often, you will find a shallow point extending out into the canal with deeper water all around it. If it is positioned in the turn, the point can be even more productive because it makes a perfect route for bass moving up or down the canal.

Another fine object is a big tree in the canal. If this form of cover is isolated, it is almost sure to produce some action. Remember, though, that boat positioning is a critical factor in this situation.

Another location to catch a number of bass is a small canal entering the main canal. Fish the center of the mouth, as well as the points on each side. Normally bass won't venture too far into a small canal (unless it's during the spawn). At that time of year, this is a great area.

Anytime you can locate a high spot along the shoreline (or just off of it) in a small canal, you have probably found the home of a largemouth. Spend the time and search out these irregular features. Your depthfinder will help you locate them and it's worth the effort to pinpoint it with marker buoys.

Locating a shallow depression running off of the banks of the canal can be a gold mine. Work the mouth of it thoroughly. This is where forage will travel in and out of the shallow areas — and bass know this.

And any out-cropping of bushes provides tremendous cover and shade. This kind of spot can produce bass throughout the day.

Always fan-cast the shoreline. This way, you will find other submerged cover that's not visible and probably more bass. Always position your boat to work into the wind, instead of drifting with it. Drifting with the wind will cause you to fish too fast and miss key areas. You will also bang into objects spooking the fish and it will be much harder to cast and control your lure properly.

Earlier, I mentioned fishing wooden objects, so let me offer some tips on fishing several of the more popular ones. As I said, of all of the objects in the water, none seem to elevate the confidence of a bass fisherman more than an exciting looking stump.

Remember that the shady side of an object is normally better than the brighter side. In fishing a target like this, it's always best to cast beyond the object so that you can cover the back, side and front with one cast. Your next cast should be to the opposite side. Many times, a bass won't be right on the stump, but near it — so making several more casts out from the stump could really pay off.

Another popular canal object is a log. Anytime you see a log along the shore with one end reaching above the surface, you can assume that the log is waterlogged on the larger end. The bass may

My buddy Tate Bowden caught this big fish in the dead-end section of a large canal.

be near the section that extends above the surface or they could be out deeper where more cover is present. As I said earlier, position your boat out where you can make parallel casts to all of the log.

Treetops can also be super objects in a canal.

Frequently, a tree blows down during a storm or erodes out and comes crashing into the water. All that remains on the bank is a stump or a short end of the tree base. Most fishermen will begin to cast around the stump and only the portion of the tree protruding above the surface — ignoring the fact that the rest of the tree and most of the cover is under the surface. The best way to fish it is to position your boat out in the deeper water and fan-cast along the length of the tree. The idea is to cast into the tree and retrieve in the direction the branches point.

By doing this, you will minimize the chances of hanging up. Never cast across the branches. If you hook a bass on the opposite side, your chances of landing it are very slim. Plus, you run the risk of possibly spooking other catchable bass that are nearby.

Canals can be outstanding out-of-the-way largemouth factories that you can enjoy all to yourself. Don't be among the countless anglers who bypass these waterways on the way to the bigger lakes.

One final thought: it is vital that you practice catch and release in these canals. Many of them are small and can quickly be fished out. Enjoy that special feeling that comes from within as you free a bass that you have just caught. As you watch it swim away, you will know that you have just made a personal contribution towards the future of bass fishing — and that fishery itself. It's like a guarantee towards tomorrow.

While it may be true that you will likely never see that particular fish again, some other angler just might. And you will almost certainly see her offspring. Then you will remember the one you released with fond memories. You will see her once again in the eyes of your mind.

The Scout is one of those older, forgotten lures. The new version with a built-in rattle is great for parallelling bluffs during the times when the bass are shallow.

Chapter 34

BLUFFS: THE INTIMIDATING STRUCTURE

Bluffs are a type of structure that is one of the most intimidating sights many bass fishermen will face when visiting a new lake. It almost always signals deeper water, which in turn means bass that are harder to catch.

The term "bluff" probably has different meanings to different people. There are sheer limestone bluffs in places like the Ozarks, which are vertical in nature. In the South in states like Georgia and Alabama, the highland reservoirs typically are mountainous terrain with a river running through that has been dammed up — water that has backed up into the high mountains and cliffs. Then there are bluffs in the lakes out West that are so sheer that the cracks in the canyon walls may be the only place for bass to hold.

Regardless of where they are located, bluffs are interesting places to fish because bass can live there throughout the year. They can move along it vertically. They can suspend shallow. They can move deep. They don't have to go far to find different depths of water to live in depending on the water temperature or different weather conditions.

By definition, bluffs are broad-based banks or cliffs made of rock, mud or clay. A feature of mainly midland and highland reservoirs, bluffs are often found where a creek or river channel washes into the bank. Most are submerged, but some can be detected by examining the shoreline. Submerged bluffs are sometimes the only irregular feature in a large section of a lake or reservoir.

These are places that most fishermen drive past because they don't look like spots that would hold concentrations of bass — but they do.

Just because the bluff is usually located next to deep water doesn't imply that the bass using it will be located deep. Bass location here depends on many different factors including shade, forage,

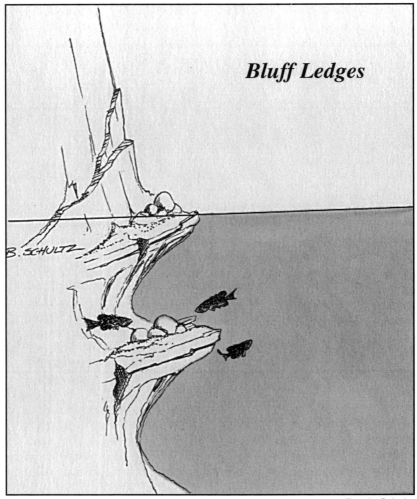

Bernie Schultz

Bluff ledges provide bass with the ideal year-round habitat. Such structure offers cover and shelter, as well as instant access to deeper water should conditions change.

current, pH, water clarity, light penetration, type of cover, substructure and irregular features. These are major guidelines to use when trying to establish a depth pattern. These factors also indicate why some bluffs are better than others.

There is really no single method for fishing bluffs on a consistent basis. This is why your approach must be varied: the bass is so unpredictable, and because of the constantly changing elements and physical configuration of some bluffs. Sure, there are certain depth and location patterns that can produce fish for a period of time, but they are always changing. One morning you might find bass suspended 5 feet deep over 60 feet of water and 15 to 20 feet out from the bluff. That afternoon, they could move from one end of the bluff to the other where the channel turns in or turns out and then settle there on a ledge or underwater bluff point 10 to 15 feet deep.

Bluffs come in all shapes, types and sizes, and are located in so many different areas. There are visible rock bluffs —some high, some steep, some low, some short, and some long. Some bluffs are laced with timber (we refer to these as timbered bluffs). You also have bluffs that are mud, clay and rock or combinations of all three. And there are submerged bluffs, those located along the submerged outside bends of the actual channel that meanders their way across the floor of the lake.

There are many good places to fish along a bluff. As I mentioned, bass location depends on several things — one being light penetration. The time of the year has a great deal to do with the amount of penetrating light. Provided there is no cloud cover, the angle of the sun is more direct on a body of water during the midday during summer months than it is during fall and winter months. The greater the angle at which light strikes the water, the more it is dispersed before it achieves any depth.

Another tip about fishing areas of this type involves clear water. Clear water is an important ingredient in how strong bluffs might be on a particular lake. In this type of environment, bass tend to move vertically more than horizontally which is another reason they seem to hold close to a bluff. As conditions change — weather, feed, light, pH, water clarity or whatever — the bass can go up or down. With other types of structure, they may move horizontally (100 yards that way or 100 yards the other way) to find suitable conditions for that particular day.

You will not find extremely clear water along every bluff that you fish, so it is important to understand water clarity. The color of the water in any given lake will determine for the most part just how far bass will move. Thus, the distance of movement is much less in dingy water than in clear water. In other words, on a clear day with high skies and good light penetration, the bass in a dark, shallow lake may move vertically only 2 to 3 feet. But that same day, bass in a deep, clear lake may be forced to move 10 to 15 feet deeper. It's not the fact that bright light hurts the fish's eye; on the contrary, it doesn't. The reason bass prefer subdued light is because they can conceal themselves and see much better to ambush their prey.

Some of the most productive bluffs are those that are basically clean bluffs featuring a series of short stairstep ledges with deep undercut sections between each ledge (which provides excellent cover and shade). One good way to tell if a bluff offers this type of terrain is by reading the structure above the water line.

You will see the effects of erosion above the waterline and the strata of rocks should tell you whether there will be ledges under the surface as well.

It's been said many times that the longer you can keep your lure in front of a fish or in the strike zone, the better the odds of it hitting the bait. That is why it is important to parallel a bluff whenever possible — at least on the pass, using a series of fan-casts. By doing this, you will be able to fish it more thoroughly and faster than by casting into it. And your lure will be in a productive zone at least 80- to 100-percent of the time.

A jig-and-pork combination, crankbait (like the Fat A or Fat Free Shad), plastic worms and grubs all have proven to be dependable lures for locating and catching bluff bass. During the times when the fish are shallow, topwater plugs, spinnerbaits and buzzbaits can be surprisingly effective.

I mentioned the word substructure earlier. Let me explain what that is. Whenever you can find structure within structure, you know it is going to be a preferred spot. This is particularly true with bluffs.

You need to look for cuts, pockets, slides or points on the bluff or at each end. Naturally, the farther these areas are apart, the better your chances of finding the fish on them. By reading the visible bluff structure, you will be able to paint a fair picture of these substructure features that extend on below the surface.

Earlier, I mentioned points at the end of the bluffs. These features are prime locations — especially if it is a channel bluff. This is where the channel comes up against it or just before the channel brushes the bank and starts to turn away. The upper end is called the turn-in and the lower portion is called the turn-out. If a current is present (either natural or caused by water being pulled from a dam or spillway downstream), you will nearly always find that the up-current point will be the most productive. To be perfectly honest, I can't tell you why, but I do know that this is true.

One of the best ways to fish a bluff is to parallel it. However, if the ledges extend way out into the lake, there are times when the only way you are going to catch fish on the bluff is to cast directly into it and work a lure like a buzzbait or topwater (if the bass are fairly shallow), worm, grub, jig and crankbait from ledge to ledge. Walking a lure down the ledge takes a certain amount of practice, feel, and skill. If you lift your rod tip too much, the lure will probably

Jerry Cockrell found this trophy sitting at the end of a bluff. A jig-and-pork chunk did the trick.

move too far and could miss the ledge. The trick is to move the lure slowly only a few inches at a time allowing it to fall to the next ledge. Fishing the lure this way and using this presentation is not the fastest fishing method ever devised, but it is an extremely effective one.

Take my advice, the next time you head out on a lake and see this type of structure, don't let it intimidate you. Instead, intimidate it. And when you do, you might just find that you have called its bluff.

Appendix

One of my biggest joys in fishing is the chance to share my love of this sport with wide-eyed kids like my grandson Chase.

CHAPTER 35

HOOKING KIDS ON FISHING

Have you ever taken a youngster fishing with you? Well, if you haven't, there is no better place than a farm pond that's overstocked with bluegill or catfish. Youngsters need enthusiasm — and a catfish tugging on the end of their line can provide plenty. The size of the fish isn't really as important to a child as just catching something.

Introducing a child to fishing is one of the greatest gifts you can provide. And it is well worth the effort.

When you do, take along just a couple of rods; that will be enough, believe me. You will be as busy as a possum or coon in a garbage can just helping your young angler. You will want to bring along something you won't find in a tackle box — a good-sized portion of old fashioned good humor and a big slice of patience.

Keep in mind that a child, whether yours or a neighbor's, will be trying hard to do the right thing. These budding anglers want to please the teacher, but need a lot of help (especially in the form of patience).

For example, just helping a child rig his or her rod, or baiting their hook may seem a little frustrating. But it can also be a lighter moment if you bring along your sense of humor.

I can tell you from experience that catching that first fish will require more patience from you than it will from the child. Trying to get the baited hook out to the right spot often isn't easy for a youngster, so you may have to help. If they don't get a bite in the first 10 seconds or so, they will probably want to reel it right back in to see if the bait is still on the hook. Children are easily distracted if the fish don't cooperate fast enough. They quickly find that it's lots of fun throwing sticks or rocks at the float — or maybe even splashing the water with their rod tip. When this begins — and believe me, it will — remember the key words: patience, patience, patience.

The real fun begins when that first fish pulls the float under. You may have to help with several suggestions at this point and possibly even net the fish, because you will have one pretty excited youngster about this time.

Catfish are a great species to launch the fishing career of an aspiring bass angler. There's no doubt that catfish can provide a ton of fun and action. Catfish feed on the bottom, but lend themselves well to float fishing. Catfish also feed at mid-range depths and even on the surface and can detect your smelly bait at almost any depth. And using a float is a terrific way to start a young fisherman because they can see a sure sign of the action taking place below the surface.

Keep reminding yourself that a younger child's attention span is shorter than yours, so you really need to be able to catch fish on a fairly regular basis. Long periods of inactivity bore small folks quickly, so try to avoid this. Fishing for trophy bass may be your thing, but most kids under the age of 12 don't have the patience for this. Each child is different, of course, so gauge accordingly.

An important point to remember is that when you take a child fishing with you, in reality you are tagging along with him or her. It's actually his show.

If the focus of attention stays on the youngster, the results will be more enjoyable for both of you. We all know that reflexes and mental keenness are usually not as well developed in children as they are in adults. Youngsters are bound to make mistakes from time to time, so it is important to try hard to maintain your composure and not lose your cool when the inevitable happens.

Quite frankly, fishing with a young child dictates that the adult angler must sacrifice a good deal. You have to strive to be patient, understanding and helpful. After all, you most likely took the young angler fishing for good reason —and I doubt if that reason was for you to catch most of the fish.

Most likely, it was for the enjoyment of the child. And when the child enjoys himself, you will join in on the fun.

It's important to always remember that a young angler can't be expected to have the ability to even come close to doing some things correctly at the beginning. Special attention, care and guidance must be given. If you handle it right, you might be lucky enough to develop a wonderful, lifetime fishing buddy. A child's life can be influenced greatly by a parent, friend or neighbor who takes the time to provide that personal direction a child so desperately needs while growing up.

There probably isn't anything better than fishing to teach the real values of true sportsmanship and develop cherished relationships.

In this day and age when kids seem to be consumed by less-healthy activities like video games and television, the sport of fishing is floundering when it comes to attracting youngsters to the wonderful pastime we know and love. Because of this, the future of fishing as we know is clouded. We have got to find ways to get more kids interested in fishing — both for each individual youngster and the sport itself.

I heard some statistics recently that indicate that if a kid has not been introduced to the sport of fishing early, the chances are poor that he or she will become very involved with it later in life. In other words, by the age of 12 they have already selected their sports. So we need to introduce these kids to our sport at a young age, say, eight to 12.

Although times are changing, that responsibility most often falls on the father. And in many cases, the father avoids any such duty because of a fear of failure. I think some fathers may be a little reluctant to go out and truly build a rapport with their sons and daughters. But that's something that needs to be done more often. This sport is a good vehicle for fathers to learn more about their sons or daughters.

And a father-son or father-daughter relationship is one of the most precious things that life has to offer.

The fondest memories of our lives occur during childhood. It is the pleasurable (and not so enjoyable) experiences that happen during our highly formative years that help shape our lives and the people that we become.

Never will our senses be as keen as they were during our most impressionable years. Never will we be as vulnerable or as open to the new experiences that life throws at us. Never will our enthusiasm be as high or as pure. Puberty may signal the beginning of the end of adolescence, but those childhood impressions stay with us forever.

Nowhere is that more evident than in the arena of youth sports.

Organized youth sports with names like Little League baseball, Pop Warner football and countless soccer and basketball leagues are a part of our heritage, the most American of traditions. Under the best of circumstances, they provide a glimpse of what it takes to become a good person and succeed at life. They help to instill the principles of self-discipline, sportsmanship and camaraderie that become so important in adulthood.

At their worst, organized youth sports can be a nightmarish experience, tearing at the confidence, self-esteem and sheer enthusiasm of our children. Such horror stories have been well-documented.

Participation in organized activities is an important part of growing up, however. Psychologists tell us that such social interaction is a vital part of learning to play the game of life. But there is an alternative that is considerably more healthy when presented in its most positive fashion.

Fishing in general is a wonderful sport for kids of all ages. Fishing provides all of the healthy, natural elements that most parents seek for their children's recreational activities. Since there are no coaches or organized fishing leagues, fishing is an activity that demands that both parent and child spend some quality time together. And that is an increasingly rare commodity in these days of dual-income families and Super-Nintendo games.

It is a recreation that takes place in some of the most wonderful places in the world, scenes where the only distraction are those natural and good. For the naturally inquisitive mind of a child, the outdoors is a magnificent playground.

And it is, generally, a low-key recreation without the ingredients of youthful anguish. There are no overbearing coaches with inflated expectations. There is no such atrocity as a strike out. There is no humiliation from getting cut — being told you are not good enough to play with your friends on an organized team. And the possibility of a physical injury is slight.

But like other sports, the introduction to fishing should not be done haphazardly. There is a definite right way to go about it and some seriously wrong ways. And that responsibility falls on the parents and other adults.

There is so much that this sport has to offer to kids, but it should be like any other sport — parents shouldn't rush them into it. The first rule of thumb involved with introducing children to fishing is to avoid creating an atmosphere similar to that found in such high-pressure, success-oriented team sports as Little League baseball. It is important that parents learn to gauge success based on the experience rather than on the number of fish a youngster catches. This was never intended to be sport with a box score.

Such pressured pitfalls can easily sour a child on fishing.

If there has been one failing from a professional standpoint, it is our emphasis on limits and big catches. Even though we didn't intend the for it to be interpreted that way, it implies to a lot of people that the only way to have a successful trip is to catch a limit. I don't think that is true. And it's especially not true with kids. It's important to teach kids to enjoy the experience of being outdoors and if you give a child the chance, he will learn that automatically.

Experience as both as an occasional guide (in the old days), father and grandfather has taught me to introduce fishing to children

Zebco/MotorGuide president Jim Dawson is the industry leader in the movement to introduce more kids to fishing.

in a slow, easy-going manner, letting the kids decide just how involved they want to be. The idea is to provide the opportunity to go fishing, offer some instruction and let the child dictate the pace.

Pace is the key. Expose a child to fishing while creating a relaxed atmosphere for learning more about it. Children, being children, often will have a limited attention span. That's fine. If the kids want to stop fishing for a while to play with the minnows, let him. If he wants to pause to swim, join him.

Children, as individuals, will choose their own pace. Some become serious, skilled anglers who will want to compete in a tournament someday. Others will go along on fishing trips, but be more interested in collecting minnows or chasing butterflies than fishing.

One of the keys to providing a warm, responsive introduction to the sport of fishing is to not concentrate on catching fish. Concentrate on the child's experience and emphasize other aspects besides the catch.

Get him or her focused on other things in fishing. Say you are fishing a Zara Spook. Forget about whether or not a fish bites it. Get the kid really involved in watching it walk down the side of a log. Get him excited about making the lure work properly. That's part of the fun of fishing. A lot of the techniques are kind of neat to do whether you get a bite or not.

Introducing kids to fishing can be a rewarding experience for all involved — adults and children alike.

I am particularly proud to be associated with Zebco and MotorGuide, a company that has been my sponsor for many years. No manufacturer has had a greater impact on the fishing youth of this country as the Zebco folks. I'm willing to bet you that 90 percent of today's adult bass anglers caught their first fish on a Zebco 303 or similar spincast outfit.

But their commitment to the youth of America goes much farther than that. You can see it in the countless hours and dollars they devote to both youth fishing and conservation projects. And they are one of the primary sponsors of the highly successful Bassmaster CastingKids program that enables young people to compete in friendly local casting contests that can ultimately lead to some major scholarship money and a trip to the BASS Masters Classic.

The folks at Zebco make it happen.

"The future of fishing depends on our ability to get the youth into the sport," advises Jim Dawson, president of Zebco/MotorGuide and my longtime friend. " We spend nearly half a million dollars each year on programs designed to be sure we have fishermen in the years ahead. And I'm not talking about in a couple of years or even five years from now. I'm talking about 15 years and beyond. Zebco's been taking kids fishing for the past 45 years and we're not going to stop now. We're in this business for the long run and that starts with today's youth."

Another reason I'm proud to be associated with this Oklahoma-based corporation is the commitment to their Made in America program. While other manufacturers were looking to make a fast buck by sending their rod- and reel-making jobs to other countries, Zebco has placed its trust in the American people.

And that makes you feel good.

"Zebco is the last major fishing tackle company left in America and we're here to stay," Dawson told me recently. "While other tackle companies are looking more and more to cheaper overseas labor sources, we're bringing jobs back to America.

"We build all of our spincast reels here. Just recently, we have started building the first baitcasting reels made in the states in nearly 15 years. We have also entered into a major 'Made in America' rod campaign. All in all, we have brought over 200 jobs back home in the past 30 months and there's going to be more. At Zebco, we believe that "Made in the USA" on a product does make a difference. Perhaps not in looks, nor in function, but certainly in character. It's a symbol that stands for quality, craftsmanship and pride. The kind of pride that built America and made her what she is today."

That's a breath of fresh air out of Corporate America folks.

When it comes to introducing the youth of this country to the life-long passion of fishing, Zebco and other companies can only do so much. It's up to each and every one of us to take the time and make the effort.

Look back on your own life. Remember that special someone who took the time to teach you and share with you the many enjoyable outdoor experiences of your youth? I would be willing to bet that this person holds a very special place in your heart.

CHAPTER 36

LEARN MORE ABOUT LARGEMOUTH BASS

RECOMMENDED BASS GUIDES

Glen Hunter, Rt. 6, Box 862, Okeechobee, FL 34974 (813-946-1569); Lake Okeechobee.

Larry Lazoen, 8 Prineville St., Port Charlotte, FL 33954 (813-627-1704). Lake Okeechobee and other south Florida waters.

Steve Daniel, P.O. Box 1972, Clewiston, FL 33440 (813-983-9271). Lake Okeechobee.

Sam Aversa, P.O. Box 1445, Hawthorne, FL 32640 (352-481-3306). Orange, Lochloosa, Rodman Reservoir and the St. Johns River.

Lou Williams, 548 Sweet Lips Road, Henderson, TN 38340 (901-989-5367). Pickwick Lake.

Terry Baksay, 339 Black Rock Road, Easton, CT 06612 (203-268-4204). Many northeastern lakes including Winnipesaukee and Candlewood.

Dave Barnes, R.R. 1, Box 2920, Weeks Mills, ME 04361 (207-445-4627). Many northeastern Lakes including Cobboseecontee and Winnipesaukee.

Todd Cronic, 5023 Gunner's Run, Roswell, GA 30075 (404-992-4635). Sinclair, Oconee, West Point and Lanier.

Ken Ellis, 1016 Striper Ave., Moncks Corner, SC 29461 (803-761-6405). Santee-Cooper Reservoir.

Bert Fischer, Roland Martin's Lakeside Resort, 920 Del Monte Ave., Clewiston, FL 33440 (813-983-3151). Lake Okeechobee and the Everglades.

Ronnie Granier, 816 Ruth Dr., Avondale, LA 70094 (504-436-0511). Mississippi Delta region.

Alton Jones, 732 Ivy Ann Dr., Waco, TX 76712 (817-751-0667). Richland-Chambers, Whitney and other Texas lakes.

Tom Mann, Jr., 5957 Lanier Heights Rd., Buford, GA 30518 (404-945-6611). Lake Lanier

Bobby Phillips, Mid-Atlantic Bass Guides, 8500 Harris Ave., Baltimore, MD 21234 (301-661-2024). Lakes and rivers in Maryland, Pennsylvania, Virginia and Delaware.

Mark Stevenson, Rt. 2, Box 280, Alba, TX 75410 (903-765-3120). Lake Fork.

Doug Youngblood, P.O. Box 1191, Buford, GA 30518 (404-945-0797). Lake Lanier.
Butch Vann, Bienville Plantation, Rt. 2, Box 262-D, Live Oak, FL 32060 (912-755-9355). Private phosphate lakes in north Florida.
Chuck Crow, 1323 Azalea Way, Winter Garden, FL 34787 (407-877-7444). Many lakes in the Orlando area.
Rick Lillegard, 21 Hemlock Heights Rd., Atkinson, NH 03811 (603-329-6438). Winnipesaukee and other northeastern lakes.

BASS ORGANIZATIONS

Bass Anglers Sportsman Society, 5845 Carmichael Road, Montgomery, AL 36117 (334-272-9530)
Operation Bass, Rt. 2, Box 74-B, Gilbertsville, KY 42044 (502-362-4304).
Bassing America, 1940 Kentwood Lane, Carrollton, TX 75005 (214-380-2656).
Angler's Choice, 1093 Fairway Dr., Granbury, TX 76049 (817-326-5821).

BASS READING

Bassmaster Magazine, 5845 Carmichael Road, Montgomery, AL 36117 (334-272-9530). The bible of America's bass fishermen.
B.A.S.S. Times, 5845 Carmichael Road, Montgomery, AL 36117 (334-272-9530). Monthly tabloid filled with the kind of information anglers crave.
Bassin' Magazine. NATCOM, Inc., 5300 CityPlex Tower, 2448 E. 81st St., Tulsa OK 74137 (918-491-6100); national magazine published bi-monthly.
North American Fisherman, 12301 Whitewater Dr., Minnetonka, MN 55343 (612-936-9333). America's largest multi-species magazine. Covers bass fishing in every issue with features, a Q & A column with their Bass Advisory Council or pros and a column co-written by Bill Dance and Roland Martin.
Bass Fishing Magazine, Operation Bass, Rt. 2, Box 74-B, Gilbertsville, KY 42044 (502-362-4304). Magazine of the Red Man Tournament Trail.
Secrets of America's Best Bass Pros and **More! Secrets of America's Best Bass Pros,** By Tim Tucker, Tim Tucker Outdoor Productions Corp., Rt. 2, Box 177, Micanopy, FL 32667 (800-252-FISH). Award-winning two-volume set that utilizes top tournament pros as sources for valuable tips, tactics and strategies. ($22.90 postpaid for two-volume set)
Diary of a Bass Pro: A Year on the Inside of Fishing's Fast Track, By Joe Thomas with Tim Tucker. Tim Tucker Outdoor Productions Corp. The first diary of a big-name bass pro, this book follows former Red Man All-American winner and four-time BASS Masters Classic qualifier Joe Thomas through an entire season on the national tournament trail. ($14.95 postpaid).
Roland Martin's 101 Bass-Catching Secrets, Tim Tucker Outdoor

Roland Martin's 101 Bass-Catching Secrets, Tim Tucker Outdoor Productions Corp. A 429-page hardback book that belongs on every angler's bookshelf. ($21.95 postpaid).

Advanced Shiner Fishing Techniques, By Glen Hunter with Tim Tucker, Tim Tucker Outdoor Productions Corp. The only book ever done on this form of live-bait fishing for trophy-sized largemouths. ($12.95 postpaid).

Catching Bass Like a Pro, By Guy Eaker and Steve Price. Eaker Books, Rt. 3, Box 255, Cherryville, NC 28021 (704-435-2116). One of the country's top pros share his tricks and tactics for locating and catching bass. A complete look at the sport — from fishing strategies to advice on turning pro, obtaining sponsors and competing in tournaments. ($11.95).

For a free copy of **Tim Tucker's Bass Catalog** (containing more than 70 books, videos, instructional audio cassettes and calendars) write to Rt. 2, Box 177, Micanopy, FL 32667 or call toll-free 800-252-FISH.

BILL DANCE'S BASS GEAR

Rods and reels: Zebco/Quantum, Zebco Corp., P.O. Box 270, Tulsa, OK 74101 (918-836-5581).

Line: Stren Fishing Lines, Delle Donne Corporate Center, 1011 Centre Road, Second Floor, Wilmington, DE 19805 (800-243-9700).

Lures. Strike King Lure Co., 174 Highway 72 West, Collierville, TN 38107 (901-853-1455). Bomber Lures and Riverside Plastics, P.O. Box 1587, Fort Smith, AR 72902 (800-422-FISH).

Trolling Motor: MotorGuide, P.O. Box 270, Tulsa, OK 74101 (918-836-5581).

Fiberglass boat: Procraft Boats, 676 Old Nashville Hwy., Murfreesboro, TN 37129 (615-890-1593

Aluminum Boat: Fisher Marine, P.O. Box 720, Murfreesboro, TN 37133 (800-552-3489).

Hooks: Eagle Claw Fishing Tackle, P.O. Box 16011, Denver, CO 80216 (303-321-1481).

Electronics: Eagle Electronics, Inc., 12000 E. Skelly Dr., Tulsa, OK 74128 (918-437-6881).

Outboard motor: Mercury Marine, P.O. Box 1939, Fond du Lac, WI 54936 (414-929-5231).

Tackle boxes: Plano, 431 E. South St., Plano, IL 60545 (708-552-3111).

Battery: SuperCrank, Action Pack and Stowaway by GNB Inc., 3340 Peachtree Road N.E., Atlanta, GA 30326 (404-231-1132).

Fish attractant: Riverside Real Baitfish, P.O. Box 1587, Fort Smith, AR 72902 (800-422-FISH).

Sunglasses: Bill Dance Sunglasses by Strike King Lure Co., 174 Highway 72 West, Collierville, TN 38107 (901-853-1455).

Personal flotation device: Stearns Manufacturing Co., 1100 Stearns Dr., Sauk Rapids, MN 56379 (800-328-3208).

Get Your Free Copy!

Tim Tucker's
Bass Catalog

The finest in instructional books, videos, audio cassettes, gifts and tournament items specially selected by Bassmaster Magazine senior writer Tim Tucker. Home of the Bill Dance Fisherman's Library!

Yes, send me my own copy!

Name _____

Address _____

City _____ State _____ Zip _____

Learn From the Pros!